Also by Martin Page

Unpersoned (with David Berg)
Kiss Me Goodnight, Sergeant Major
The Songs and Ballads of World War II
The Company Savage
The Lost Pleasures of the Great Trains

For Gawdsake Don't Take Me!

The Songs, Ballads, Verses, Monologues, etc. of the Call-Up Years, 1939-1963

Edited by Martin Page

Illustrated by Bill Tidy

Hart-Davis, MacGibbon London

Granada Publishing Limited
First published in Great Britain 1976 by Hart-Davis, MacGibbon Ltd
Frogmore, St Albans, Hertfordshire AL2 2NF and
3 Upper James Street, London W1R 4BP

ISBN 0 246 10859 2

Filmset in Photon Imprint 11 on 13 pt by
Richard Clay (The Chaucer Press), Ltd, Bungay, Suffolk
and printed in Great Britain by
Fletcher & Son Ltd, Norwich

Editor's Note

It is impossible adequately to thank the many scores of ex-servicemen in Britain, Australia, Canada, New Zealand, South Africa and elsewhere who together wrote this book.

If they hadn't kept for all these years the songs, ballads, verses and so on that they'd heard while they were in the forces, the book could not have existed at all.

In their honour—and in that of the men, often unknown, who originated much of the material that came to me indirectly, and many of whom are by now dead—a substantial proportion of any royalty payments received from the publishers will be paid to charities.

For Catherine

Contents

Call Up

What did you join the army for?
Why did you join the army?

asked the mocking song that used to resound
in British army billets around the world,

What did you join the army for?
You must have been FUCKING WELL BARMY!

Whether they were barmy or not—the armed forces didn't seem to care much either way—some four million of the Britons who sang it had had no say in the matter. It had been their fate to have been male, born some time between 1902 and 1943, minimally fit, at least marginally more intelligent than a half-wit, not to have been working down a mine or on the land or a fishing trawler, and not to have had a widowed mother who would have been left penniless if her son had been called away.

The first of them received their one-way rail warrants and call-up papers ordering them through the barrack gates to get fell in, in the spring of 1939, just before World War II began. It wasn't until almost a quarter of a century later, eighteen years after that particular war to end all wars had ended, that 23819209 Private Woods,* Britain's last conscript soldier, was let back into civvy street after a two-year stint peeling potatoes in the Catering Corps, on 7 May 1963. During those twenty-four years sons of earlier conscripts were conceived, grew up and in their turn celebrated their eighteenth birthdays by coughing twice, giving a urine sample, pulling apart the cheeks of their buttocks to reveal their anuses and reporting to the training depot.

It was this often reluctant 'shower', as the regulars called them, who did most of the fighting across North Africa and through Italy, from the Normandy beaches to the Rhine and in South-east Asia in World War II, and then in Korea and in Britain's more private wars in Cyprus, Kenya and Malaya.

---

* Fred Woods, who now lives in Nantwich, Cheshire, has helped me with the compilation of this book, and has made several valuable contributions.

For Gawdsake Don't Take Me! is a collection of the disrespectful, bawdy, poignant, sardonic, subversive and other songs, verses, comic monologues and the like which came out of putting two generations of civilian men into uniform and chucking them into the alien world of drill sergeants, kit inspections, soggy fritters and shots fired in anger.

The aim of the book is not just to bring back memories to those who were called up (I have no doubt that some would rather not be reminded), but to convey to others something of what it was like to be in the forces involuntarily, in the words of those who were, as they spoke and sung them at the time.

I collected the material over eighteen months, mostly by writing to local newspapers around Britain and in Australia, New Zealand and South Africa, appealing to anyone who had done compulsory military service to send me any songs etc. that they could still remember.

The response was astonishing. Replies poured in from Aberdeen in Scotland to Toowoomba in Australia, and a few score points inbetween. There were items recalled and written out again specially for me. There were tattered scraps of paper, worn at the folds, that had been scribbled upon in a military billet just before lights out thirty years or more ago, and now retrieved from some box in an attic. There were verses and monologues that were still being privately circulated among ex-servicemen, having been freshly typed and duplicated for the purpose.

It was clear that all this time after its actual abolition, call-up was still very much alive in the minds of many of the men who went through it.

Indeed, no less than fourteen different people sent me the monologue, *'Arpin'*, which appears on page 125 of this book, about the serviceman who went to Heaven and became an Acting Angel, 3rd Class, only to find that even in the Base Camp in the Sky there is no escape from military routine for those who have been subject to it on earth:

'And the Seraph-Major gets us fell in and starts telling off parties from the right. "'Ere to 'ere, Pearly Gates polishin' party. 'Ere to 'ere, Fiery Chariots wheel greasin'. Remainder, 'arpin' . . ."'

Although many of the pieces in this book will be nostalgically familiar to countless ex-servicemen, almost none of them has ever been published before.

In some instances, there is no mystery as to why they have not been printed until now—until recently they were considered to be unprintable.

I make no apology for breaking this long-standing taboo. These pieces are not pornographic, however explicit they may be. Countless respectable citizens who have been in the forces know one or more of them by heart, and, given the slightest opportunity, recite them. No one has yet been depraved or corrupted as a result, and no one could possibly be so. What they are is bawdy, and the worst harm that they can do is to offend against some people's idea of acceptable good taste.

Others, I hope, will be pleased that these well-known classics of military ribaldry have been written down and printed at last, while their perpetrators could still remember the words. Quite apart from their entertainment value, they comprise a fascinating record of what those who defended Britain sang, recited and laughed at while they did so.

They are of more than light-hearted interest. The British conscript's penchant for bawdy rather than patriotic songs became, albeit unintentionally, one of our more bizarre secret weapons in World War II. In the early stages of the war, German agents in Cairo, hearing the British, Australians and New Zealanders singing *You can't fuck Farida if you don't pay Farouk*, *The Ball of Kirriemuir* and other disrespectful, decadent ditties, reported to Berlin that almost to a man they were too dissolute and lacking in patriotic fibre to be a match even for the Italians. This pleasing misunderstanding of national character helped delay the arrival of Rommel and the Afrika Korps and played a real if small part in the eventual defeat of the Axis powers.

It is, indeed, a striking fact that one can search this book from cover to cover without finding even the most trifling evidence of any patriotic fervour among our conscripted fighting men. This is not because I have suppressed it out of some perverse motivation of my own, but rather because none of the scores of contributors who provided the material for this book could think of any.

. . . hearing the British, Australians and New Zealanders singing disrespectful, decadent ditties . . .

'Halloo Berlin . . . The village blacksmith, he was there . . .'

On the contrary, a few of the songs that some of them sang during the war were actually subversive, and a selection of these is to be found on pages 137–41 of this book. They included *Uncle Joe*, a jolly hymn in praise of Stalin, which placed Churchill on the same moral level as Hitler, as an imperialistic warmonger.

It is perhaps a peculiarly British style of contradictory behaviour that the men who held such views, when it came to it, fought and fought bravely for Churchill's Britain. If foreigners didn't understand it, that was their loss.

There are also in this book many verses testifying that even those who had little time for barrack-room Bolshevism (the great majority, of course) were more inclined to grouse than to cheer themselves into the fray with jingoistic ballads of the kind the Germans and the Russians went in for. Some of the complaints they voiced in song can shock one even today, reflecting as they did their all too plausible conviction that the Government was taking liberties with their lives that were unwarranted even in time of war. To the men concerned, for example, it seemed a callous irony that the authorities should spend so much money training them to be navy pilots, only to imperil and in many cases lose their lives not by exposing them to the enemy but by equipping them with horrendously ill-designed, cumbersome and un-airworthy machines.

Weighs six tons, no front guns,
Fuck all to rely on.
You know what you can do
With your Barracuda II.
Old iron, old iron!

There was a whole litany of abuse for those particular planes (see pages 70–73) sung by the men who risked their necks in them. To many people today it may seem almost incredible that they didn't just refuse to fly the damned things: instead, they vented their grievances in the wardroom and, thus purged, climbed back into the cockpits.

Conversely, however, many of the grouses aired in these pages may well seem to those who weren't there extraordinarily trivial, given that there was a war on. For example, here is a man called by his country in its darkest hour to rise up and vanquish an evil enemy, complaining about the inadequate provisions for cigarette breaks during basic training:

> *. . . After a while we get a short break*
> *For five or ten minutes when we may take a smoke*
> *Just when we've lit up—one match does us all—*
> *Instructor disturbs us as he starts to bawl:*
> *'Time's up. Smokes out', in a way meant to irk.*

While men were deliriously gasping for water under the blazing sun in the Western Desert, others in Aldershot were moaning about the price of beer and the quality of their three daily meals:

> *The porridge burnt, the bacon raw,*
> *And stewed tea! No one asks for more . . .*
> *. . . Spuds and cabbage both underdone—nothing new—*
> *With gravy like water, rice lumpy, beef tough,*
> *Perhaps to convince you, I've said quite enough.*

And while some were laying down their lives in the Western Desert, others were beefing about the poor postal service for troops:

> *The mail comes to us regular,*
> *So the papers say.*
> *But the chaps who write this trash*
> *Never come our way.*

Throughout the holocaust of World War II, as battles raged and cannons roared, there they were, griping about drill and bull, about having to get up early in the morning and not getting enough holidays. Was it all, it must be asked, merely another manifestation of the world-renowned, whingeing, British bloody-mindedness?

I believe it was not. Rather it added up, first, to frustration that, having been called upon to fight a war, they found themselves occupied, in many cases for months and even years, with futile military rituals: and second, that the nation as a whole took their sacrifice of several years out of their young lives far too much for granted—that they were not given the respect and appreciation that civilians owed them.

They felt, and it would be hard indeed to gainsay them, that if their country expected them to risk their lives in its defence, the least it could do in return would be to provide such small appurtenances as edible food, that if their careers and home lives were to be disrupted it was unreasonable that this should be done just so that few regular officers and NCOs could bugger them about on a barrack square, and that if they were sent thousands of miles from home to fight and quite possibly die in a foreign desert so that the English way of life might be preserved, the rest of the country might have bothered a bit more about seeing that they got letters from home regularly.

In other words, it was not the fact that they had to fight they resented but that they felt ill used, that advantage was being taken of them.

These sentiments were to a substantial degree the product of a well-intentioned official propaganda campaign that misfired. To reassure parents and wives that their men were being cared for by the army as well as was possible, newspapers carried reports, week after week and month after month, eulogising the fine facilities there were for them. These newspapers eventually came into the hands of the men themselves, who laughed with justified bitterness, as they ate their dry biscuits and eked out their water ration, at the reports that they breakfasted daily on eggs and bacon.

They would probably have put up with the discomforts themselves with the minimum complaint, as part of the exigencies of war. But to be told then that they were being mollycoddled, in effect, was just downright insulting. And knowing that civilians back home innocently believed them to be living it up abroad made them extremely angry. Many a war correspondent in North Africa was roundly abused for his attempts to reassure the home front that conditions were as good as could be.

It was true, and in the circumstances unavoidable, that some civilians had a grotesquely exaggerated view of what life was like in the forces. Not only did it say in the papers that they were cocooned with comforts. They were regularly called upon to make sacrifices in terms of forsaking minor luxuries—marmalade, whisky, razor blades—so that these could be allocated to the troops. Lady Astor, too, played a part by campaigning in and out of Parliament against drinking and womanising among the troops, thus propagating the belief that they were being lavished with the wherewithal to conduct such activities.

Many was the man who came home on leave expecting, if not a hero's welcome, at least a grateful and respectful one, only to find himself regaled with tales of civilian deprivations for the sake of the troops, and the assumption that the latter were living the life of Reilly. One of the pieces in this book describes how, after years of waiting for home leave from North Africa, the author got his 'green signal':

Then you reach old England
And strange enough you find
There is no thrill of welcome
From those you left behind.

The contributors to this book groused a lot about their time in the forces—and no wonder. It was not the fact that they had to go and fight a war that soured them, it was the thought that they were not appreciated.

But this sourness is only one of the aspects of conscription that the contributions evoke. Perhaps most of those who served compulsorily would not admit to having enjoyed it that much, whether they served in the war or afterwards, whether they spent their time machine-gunning German positions or cleaning latrines on Salisbury Plain, providing EOKA terrorists with a walking target on Nicosia's Murder Mile or dispensing gin and tonic in the officers' mess in Ipoh, Malaya. But, as is demonstrated by the fact that this compilation has been possible, it was for almost all of them an unforgettable experience, and it was by no means all of it bad.

1

You, You and You

'Call up my brother,
My sister or my mother
But for Gawdsake don't take me.'

If those who were called up went with any degree of enthusiasm, most concealed it perfectly. In accordance with that traditional British maxim, *never volunteer for anything*, keenness to join up and fight for King and Country marked a man out as a figure of fun and derision; and those who had allegedly succeeded in outwitting the powers-that-be into debarring them from the forces were covert heroes among men of conscriptable age.

There was never any British equivalent of the New York School for Draft-Evaders. Founded in 1942 by the fabled Brooklyn con-man Julius Meyer, this did a flourishing business in one-day, fifty-dollar courses in the simulation of debilitating ailments for men about to appear before medical boards. After seven weeks the authorities caught up with Meyer and sent him to jail (by which time several hundred students had graduated). But as early as 1939, our island's grapevine was buzzing with advice—much of it grotesque—as to how to get oneself rejected; and this flow of subversive counsel was not to cease until conscription itself did.

In the early days, before Russia entered the war and was still proclaiming its pact with the Nazis, there was rumoured to be a stallholder in Petticoat Lane who sold genuine, back-dated Communist Party membership cards, with blank name-spaces; if there was, the police never caught him.

Other recourses that were urged upon the reluctant then and later were more extreme—borrowing a sewing needle from your mother and perforating your ear-drums with it, staring at the sun so as to burn holes in the retinas of your eyes, drinking your own urine so as to appear diabetic.

There were at least a dozen versions of the story of the man who feigned short-sightedness. Told to go through the door into the eye-testing room, he asked, 'What door?' Once inside, told to sit down on the chair, he asked, 'What chair?' Once sat down, told to look at the chart on the wall, he asked, 'What wall?'

Once rejected, he went to the pictures and was thoroughly enjoying the film until he noticed sitting right next to him the doctor who had given him his eye test. Quick as a flash, he turned to him and said, 'Excuse me, sir, does this bus go to Peckham?'

Needless to say, the examining doctors were soon familiar with the repertoire of medical counterfeisance played before them daily, and inured to the pleadings of those who hopefully proffered one physical shortcoming or another that they had only just discovered in themselves, to the point of winning a reputation for callousness. It was said that one man demonstrated that his left leg was two and a half inches shorter than his right one, to be told: 'You'll find that's an advantage where you're going. The fighting's over uneven ground.' Months and even years after they had joined in the battle of wits with the examining doctors, men in military billets would vie to show off to one another the bodily defects which, in their view, should have barred them from being there at all.

In retrospect, none of this should be taken too much at face value. Artful dodgers there were who got away with it, and subsequently deserters too. But these were, in the event, remarkably few in number; and if one looks at their cases individually, one finds at least as often as not that they were motivated by reasons which, while the powers-that-be didn't have them written down in their rule book as valid grounds for exemption, they themselves, not necessarily dishonourably, considered compelling. Often it was a fragile marriage which they felt would break up if they went away, or the fear of abandoning their children to the sole care of an over-harsh and insufficiently loving mother, or the knowledge that without him the family which they would have to leave behind would be incapable of running the small business on which it depended for its livelihood.

The great majority of the rest merely went through the motions of resisting call-up, for no more subversive reason than that it was the accepted form to do so. Their outward bad grace was more than anything else but an historic instance of the enjoyment the British get from pretending that they neither want to do nor can do almost anything that is asked of them, no matter how reasonably and urgently. The doing of it then becomes something of a joke at the expense of those they told it couldn't be done. And in this case, what they did was to win a war or two.

. . . would vie to show off to one another the bodily defects . . .

For Gawdsake Don't Take Me!, the title song of this book, is perhaps the finest example existing of the self-mockery of the British over their show of reluctance to rouse themselves even to repel a would-be invader.

For Gawdsake don't take me

Call up the Army and the Navy!
Call up the rank and file!
Call up the gallant territorials—
They'll save England with a smile!
Call up the boys and the old diehards
To fight so England can be free!
Call up my brother,
My sister or my mother
But for Gawdsake don't take me!

Onward, Conscript Soldiers!

The following sardonic couplet is of Australian origin (it was submitted by a prominent politician there who prefers not to be named) and shows that the British attitude towards call-up was not exclusively British.

To the tune of 'Onward Christian Soldiers'

Onward conscript soldiers, marching as to war!
You'd all be dead men now, if you'd volunteered before.

What Did You Join the Army For?

Even after enlistment any outward show of enthusiasm remained bad form, provoking mockery from one's comrades-in-arms. The conscripts regularly received pep-talks from officers, delivered with the worthy intention of instilling morale. They themselves told each other jokes that depicted willing servicemen as moronic, or at best simple-minded. For example:

A conscripted milkman writing home to his mother: 'I really like it in the army. It's so nice to lie in bed until half-past five in the morning.'

After a month in the army, a conscript was summoned by his sergeant and asked why he never attended pay parade.

'You don't mean to say that I get paid as well?' he replied in amazement.

To the tune of 'Here's to the Maiden of Bashful Fifteen'

What did you join the army for?
Why did you join the army?
What did you join the army for?
You must have been fucking well barmy!

I wanna go Home

They say that in the Army
The beds are very fine
But how the hell should they know?
They've never slept in mine.

CHORUS:
Gee ma, I wanna go
But they won't let me go
Gee ma, I wanna go home.

They say that in the Army
The food is very fine
But the bread it tastes like sawdust,
The tea's like iodine.

CHORUS

They say that in the Army
The pay is very fine
They give you forty shillings
And take back thirty-nine.

CHORUS.

Forty-nine and in the Army

Nobody who was anything like forty-nine years old was called up, of course. But this song raised laughs about the fitness of some of those who were dragged into the net.

Forty-nine and in the army,
Forty-nine and fit and fine,
Though I'm wheezy about the chest
And I'm gouty about the knees,
I'm learning to shoulder arms
Though I'm better at stand-at-ease.

Forty-nine and in the army,
I'm longing to be in the firing line,
So, if somebody holds me rifle
While I go and borrow a pair of steps,
I'll be over the top, my lads, at forty-nine.

Carlisle

They say that Carlisle is a marvellous place,
But the organisation's a fucking disgrace.
They stand on the square and they bawl and they shout.
They shout about things they know fuck-all about.
If I had my way, they would all of them be
Shovelling shit on the Isle of Capri.

Cobbers

There were those—perhaps more Australians and New Zealanders than British—who were moved by the thought that they had been called up to offer themselves, if need be, for the ultimate sacrifice, as the verse below demonstrates.

But the song *I Don't Want My Name on a Cenotaph* achieved somewhat greater popularity. The Rev. Lord Beaumont, who sent it to me, first heard it being bellowed in a sergeants' mess in Germany, some time after the war had ended.

If there's a trip one way, he said,
Into battle grim for me,
Don't let them say when I am dead:
He died to save democracy;
Nor let them say: He fought to free
Enslaved nations, white or brown;
Just print these simple words for me:
He would not let his cobbers down.

I don't want my name on a Cenotaph

To the tune of 'The Eton Boating Song'

Oh I don't want my name on a cenotaph,
In letters of shining gold.
For that won't be much use to me
When I'm lying stiff and cold.
Let the others all laugh at me
And say that I was afraid.
It is I who will have the last laugh—
I'll be first on the last parade.

I'll stay up all the night before
For I know that I shan't sleep.
I'll polish my brasses, shine my boots,
Fold my bed up nice and neat.
And early the next morning
I'll be ready with a nice clean shave.
There'll be plenty of competition,
But I'll be first on the last parade.

And when this war is over
And we've all got a nice big ale,
And when it comes round to my turn
To pay for drinks and to tell the tale,
I'll tell thefn the old story
How through mud and blood I did wade
But Sergeant will shout: 'You liar!
You were first on the last parade.'

The National Servicemen's Anthem

Towards the end of the call-up era, honour virtually disappeared and gave way to very real resentment and bitterness. The war against the Nazis had been won by men whose sons were now of military age. An attack from Russia seemed utterly implausible, with Stalin not only dead but removed from the mausoleum on Red Square and placed in an obscure grave, and the ebullient Krushchev hosting SuperMac and preaching peaceful coexistence. Britain's latest armed conflict had been the Suez fiasco, from which a handful of reservist national servicemen had absented themselves, sending telegrams expressing such sentiments as 'Up yours'.

The high command itself was fed up with conscripts, and was pressing the Government to give it a smaller but professional army. And by the early 1960s, the conscripts themselves were fed up to the teeth with being forced to give up two of the best years of their lives, learning how to impose order over a non-existent empire and to defend Britain against imaginary enemies.

Before he took up the religious vocation he now follows, the Rev. D. M. P. Giles of Guildford was an instructor in the Education Corps.

He writes: 'In 1960–62, the favourite National Service expressions were "Discontent" and "Hate". These were written in symbolic form, the symbols being:

= disc-on-tent

= H8 = Hate

'They appeared in the most unlikely places. It was not unusual to move the blackboard in a classroom and find that one of the symbols had been written on the wall behind it between lessons.'

This, then, was what many national servicemen of that period called their anthem.

How I hate the fucking Army (Air Force/Navy).
How I hate it more than I can say.
All I long for is my freedom.
Roll on, roll on, demob day.

2

A Day in the Life of a Squaddy

Harold Smith of Kettering was called up in 1940 to become a private in the Royal Northumberland Fusiliers. A few weeks after he had left home, his wife sent him a letter asking him what it was *really* like to be in the army.

At the time, newsreels and photo-features in the illustrated magazines were showing the conscript soldiers racing each other like exuberant grown-up schoolboys across obstacle courses, singing heartily together on route marches, staging mock battles 'somewhere in England', wiping out an imaginary regiment or two of Germans before lunchtime, and then gleefully tucking in to their plentiful, wholesome grub served by smiling cookhouse orderlies.

Private Smith wrote for his wife a series of letters in verse, presenting army life as it was with the propagandists' varnish stripped off. She kept them, and when Harold returned from the war, he put them together to form a continuous verse narrative which he called *A Day in the Life of a Squaddy*. A friend typed it out for him, and he had copies made for the enlightenment and amusement of his family and friends.

It is printed here for the first time, and it is a rarity to be treasured. Good-humoured and free from any taint of bitterness, but pulling no punches, it is a unique and authentic account of the everyday trials and tribulations of a conscript soldier—written at the time and on the spot without the benefit, or rather the distortions of hindsight that mar most other accounts.

A Day in the Life of a Squaddy

Deeply I sleep, or do I—I wonder—
Make noises strange, and loud as thunder.
However, I then have a dream
That's oft repeated and it would seem
The cause is not so hard to find.
It's the orderly sergeant's 'Do you mind,
Please getting up. It's seven, I think.
FEET OUT, OR ELSE YOU'LL BE IN CLINK.'

We put our feet out of the bed,
As the OS looks and shakes his head
But when he's safely through the door
We dive back in for five minutes more.
Then if the OS should return
By devious ways we've come to learn
His presence with a minute to spare,
So we all put on an innocent air.

But now get up we really must,
Set up our beds and sweep and dust.
Our beds in which we take great pride,
All look so neat as side by side
They're levelled up and then dressed off,
And all looks perfect till a cough
From I/C room warns something's wrong,
In language perhaps a little strong.

At last the room is all put straight,
But breakfast for us will not wait.
First wash and shave before we eat
So with the rush of many feet

Into the wash house we all pour
Nearly smashing down the door.
Two wash bowls do us, forty blokes.
The cause of scraps as well as jokes.

At last we're clean. Ablutions done,
We go to breakfast one by one,
The porridge burnt, the bacon raw.
And stewed tea! No one asks for more.
However, no one blames the cooks,
Except by casting dirty looks.
When orderly officer asks 'All right?'
We answer 'Yes Sir,' so polite.

Breakfast over, we sit awhile,
Discussing things that make us smile.
Officers and NCOs
The MG* and all that with it goes.
And having, too, a quiet sly smoke—
To be caught at this is not a joke.
Well, time to leave dining hall, and
Walk out with fag cupped in one's hand.

Next we come to muster parade,
For which sergeant-majors are specially made.
We shuffle about and line up in threes
We come to attention, then stand at ease.
The OC appears, then attention once more,
As with sergeant-major he starts on his tour.
To sort out good from bad in ranks.
Though he's never yet been known to say thanks.

* Machine gun.

He stumbles up one row then down the next.
Checks haircuts, loose buttons, but only he's vexed.
At last with a sigh we realise he's through
Even so, for him, we never seem to do.
Sergeant-major takes over, looking frightfully stern,
Raps out an order that makes our ears burn,
'Shun' salutes OC, then turns round to us
And details us off, without any fuss.

'You, you and you, on grenades for today,
And you lot there on MG'—that's the way
That we are told our jobs, some better than others,
By the bloke they say takes the place of our mothers.
Away we all go in little squads,
With NCOs feeling like little tin gods.
It's as well they do, and don't realise
They're really inferior to us other guys.

Of training itself I needn't say more,
For it wouldn't interest you, I'm sure.
That it bores some of us you need not doubt
Though we often catch the instructor out.
On such like occasions he resorts to his book,
And attempts to give us a knowing look,
Until the book has proved him wrong,
When he skips the subject that proved too strong.

Now after a while we get a short break
For five or ten minutes when we may take
A smoke—that is, if we have any fags
Or can borrow some from the bloke who has bags.
Just when we've lit up—one match does us all—
Instructor disturbs us as he starts to bawl:
'Time's up, smokes out' in a way meant to irk,
Just fancy him thinking we'd try to shirk.

Somehow we manage until the big break,
Half an hour in Naffi now we may take.
With warning from corporal 'Be back on the dot,
Or a charge you'll be on, the whole bloody lot'
We race to the Naffi to be first in the queue,
Though cakes not much good and tea's a poor brew.
And when we are served we sit round and talk,
Till times up, then back to instructor we walk.

From big break to dinner we seldom do much:
The break it appears has made us lose touch,
Excepting for musketry—bane of us all—
Another fine chance for instructors to bawl
''Port arms, examine arms, ease springs, order arms.'
How well they demonstrate their vocal charms.
Still we're not affected, our minds think as one
Of getting our dinner, getting rid of our gun.

At last we're dismissed, away we all go,
To put up our rifles in row after row.
Next to the billet, for knife, fork and spoon
To the dining hall then—not a moment too soon.
The queue is already a considerable size
You'd think it a meal the fellows all prize.
But that's a mistake I can soon rectify,
Come, look in the swill bin that goes to our sty.

Of the menu today the cooks perhaps boast
Potatoes and cabbage and gravy and roast.
And, of course, a sweet—the eternal rice—
But if you're thinking that all this is nice
I'll tell you the truth without more ado:
Spuds and cabbage both underdone—nothing new—
With gravy like water, rice lumpy, beef tough
Perhaps to convince you, I've said quite enough.

Of course, orderly officer comes round to see
If there's any complaint, but the answer that we
Always give is the same 'No complaints sir', Why?
The effect's just the same so no harm's in the lie,
So once more to Naffi all of us go
For more tea and fags and general pow-wow
Till at one forty-five we parade yet once more,
Though the turn-out now looks very poor.

There are less on parade than at nine today,
But that is expected, for some have a way
Of dodging parade with excuse watertight—
After two years of service, they're past masters, quite.
This time no inspection, we're soon marched away.
Again we're in squads so no one can stray,
But instructor may yet lead to some grassy slope
Where, secluded, we'll scrounge till teatime—we hope.

However, the training goes on as before
Although we're browned off and it's all such a bore,
With occasional breaks for a smoke now and then.
We wish time away until four fifteen, when
We're sent off to billets and all told to strip
Get PT kit on—now we've all got the pip,
The reason? Well, everyone dislikes PT,
And to get off it we use any old plea.

Some hide in one place and some in another
Excepting the privileged who don't need to bother.
If you'd like to know I'll describe what it's like
And without exaggerating or taking the Mike.
Parade company lines, first we are told.
So we make our way there shivering with cold,
And stand there in threes with ten minutes to spare,
Till someone decides we should be on the square.

We march on to markers, dress off from the right
Five companies are there, what a perishing sight.
Bare legs and arms, all blue with the cold,
While OS reports to RSM—so bold,
He's never been seen in PT kit yet
And never will be, that's a good bet.
Eventually the RSM starts the fun,
With 'Right turn', 'Double', away we run.

Sometimes we do exercises. To me they're just rot.
They're seldom done properly, so most prefer a trot
Which at least helps us to get warm once again,
And that way we finish before time—quite a gain.
When the period's over we rush off to change
Showing energy both amazing and strange.
In no time we're washed and dressed in BD
Queued up in dining hall and waiting for tea.

Tea's not too bad with fish, bread and marge,
Though the portions allowed are not very large,
The tea's not much good, while the bread's rather stale,
The fish so much off, one dare not inhale.
Well, so much for tea with all its distractions
We'll soon be away seeking different attractions
For most of us have the same object in view:
To get out with all speed seeking pleasures anew.

Of course, there's the flicks where all of us go,
But we can't go there six nights in a row.
Our pay's insufficient though some say we're well paid,
They're the ones when we're broke don't come to our aid.
The girls attract some blokes to such an extent
Their intentions one might say are hardly well meant.
But, perhaps that's enough of what fills our spare time.
Discretion, in that respect, must temper my rhyme.

Harold Smith

MP

3

Our Jim

'The fucking thing was ours.'

Summoned by the King to go and rout the Nazi menace on behalf of himself and democracy, you shook hands with your father, man-to-man for the first time. Your mother wept proud tears. Your younger brother gazed up at you with envy and new-found respect. And, third-class rail warrant in hand, you went.

Six weeks later, after basic training, you were the master of the bayonet, the rifle and the mortar, physically fit as never before, and as ready as you would ever be to go into action.

The Germans had by now swept across Europe from the Atlantic to the Mediterranean. In North Africa, Britain and the allies were fighting a one-from-last-ditch stand to save Egypt and Palestine. In Burma, we were making our determined stand against the Japanese advance through Asia. Over England itself, the fighter pilots of the RAF daily locked themselves in heroic combat with the marauding Luftwaffe.

And you? If you were lucky enough not to be peeling spuds in the middle of Salisbury Plain, you were quite likely standing on the shingle beach at Hastings staring out into the Channel, just in case a canoe full of German invaders came your way, or manning an anti-aircraft artillery post in a desolate south-eastern suburb over which an enemy aircraft had not yet been known to fly, and where the only major event so far had been the sergeant's trousers falling down as he saluted the inspecting officer's disappearing car. It wasn't, to put it mildly, much to write home about, even if you had been allowed to.

Nobody was more deeply impressed by the ironic situation of these men, sent off from home as heroes on their way to great military conquests, than they were themselves. It was their sense of military futility that led them to write the cod epics of absurd, fantastical exploits enacted in their sarcastic imaginations by those who, like themselves, served by standing and waiting and then standing and waiting some more.

Our Jim

Another Heinkel hit the dust, or rather hit the sea,
Good shooting on our Jim's part, folks, I think you will agree.
The Sergeant cried: 'Cigar or nuts?' Said Jim, 'I want no prize.
This bomber I intend to fly—that is, if she will rise.'
He duffed his clothing in a flash, and swam out with a crawl,
He dumped the Nazis overboard, then did an overhaul.
'Come back! Come back!' the Sergeant cried,
'I fear that you'll be wrecked.'
Said Jim: 'Please don't distress yourself,' or words to that effect.
He flew to Berlin right away, then hovered over Munich.
By way of extra camouflage, he donned a Nazi tunic.
He landed in the castle grounds; arrived in time for lunch
With Hitler, Goering, Goebbels, Hess and all that nasty bunch.
Asked Jim, 'You blokes would like a flight?' They answered, 'Ya! Heil! Hoch!'
Said Jim, 'Well hurry. Shut your mouths, or in them put a sock!'
He shot his bomber up aloft and o'er the North Sea sped.
'Turn back!' they screamed. But Jim just laughed,
'Cheer up, you'll soon be dead.'
He landed them at Gravesend, a name that does sound grim.
His Colonel cried, 'Well done, my boy,' which did embarrass Jim.
'A VC you deserve, my lad, for capturing these mutts.'
But Jim said: 'Sir, I'd much prefer a few cigars and nuts.'

Pte. Miller, 10th West Yorks. Regt.

The Fucking Thing was Ours

The night was dark and stormy,
The wind was blowing strong,
As we sat in our hutment
While a gunner sang a song.
We were in the open country
With some ack-ack guns as hosts
When we heard an order shouted,
And straightway we took posts.
We heard a plane approaching
And thought about our town,
And how the folks would treat us
If we should bring it down.
The lights from nearby sprang up
And felt around the sky,
Like the feelers of an octopus
And we all wondered why.
With all of them above us
(they seemed to fill the air)
They never seemed to show them
To the officers standing there.
Then we had the order
And the guns all opened fire.
The noise was so terrific
As the plane went soaring higher.
We blazed away for minutes
And it seemed to stick it all
When with a cheer we saw it
Lurch sideways, and then fall.
It came crashing down towards us.
We saw it was afire.
And as it crashed behind us
The flames went roaring higher.
We ran towards it, stood stock still,
After firing there for hours.
We saw the marks upon its side—
The fucking thing was ours.

Young Albert

At Buckingham Palace, in London,
Where King and his Missus hang out,
Young Albert the Engineer went for a do.
There was champagne and oysters and stout.

Now Albert, he was a hero,
And many a brave deed had done;
With his stick with the horse's head handle,
The Battle of Dunkirk he'd won.

The ship which bore Albert to glory
Was His Majesty's trawler, *Lord Grey*,
And over the ocean he steamed in her
A-knocking and pulsing her way.

And sometimes the engines would falter
And steamboat would stop with a bump
But with horse's head handle he'd fix it
And muck up the leave, like a chump.

When Winston got wind of his actions
At Zeebrugge, Dunkirk and Bordeaux,
He asked that t'King, as a favour,
A medal on Albert bestow.

When the King saw young Albert at Palace,
To the Queen he turned round and said: 'Lass,
Yon must be young Albert what's winning t'war,
Put the lad some champagne in a glass.'

As the King was the medal about to bestow
With gesture both noble and great,
Young Albert, with stick held tight in his hand,
Said: 'Thanks King. Meet Murdo the mate.'

As Mate told t'King the full story
Of how Albert was winning the war,
Young Albert was winking at Lady Ramsbottom,
What he'd met at t'King's Head before.

On Albert's chest dangles a medal
All shiny and gradely and new
Which he wears on his suit with gold badges
From Fleming's at two pounds two.

And now when he visits the King's Head,
Where once he'd partake of a stout,
He gets Guinness and potted meat sandwiches
And pasties and trotters for nowt.

The Christmas Pud

Now the Colonel's brow was sad, and the Colonel's language low,
As darkly glowered he at the cooks, and darkly at the foe.
'The flaming joint's surrounded—the situation tough—
Oh who will race to Divvy Base and fetch a Christmas duff?'

Then up spake three Bold Babblers—and you know what Babblers are.
Craftsmen quaint, with a patron saint named Caesare Borgia,
'Though Jerries grim surround us and make the going tough
We don't give a fock (sic) for old Van Bock . . . we'll fetch a Christmas duff.'

Oh there was Milligan Murphy, OC beef and spuds,
And Cuthbert Camp, who held the champ for peeling Captain Bloods,
Bagpipe McOatmeal—late of Clyde—roared 'Aye, we'll do oor stoof,
For bide a wee, and we'll gang free and lug yon Christmas doof.'

Milligan Murphy set his course by the light of the Polar Star,
Cuthbert C. stole brazenly a Jerry armoured car.
Thumbing a lift with a Fritz patrol, McOatmeal muttered 'Guid!
Ah've saved a fare and Ah ken where I'll find yon Christmas pud.'

Oh dawn on Christmas morning (just as the poets think):
A sky of blue or green tints too and a delicate elephant
pink,
Yawning graves and a firing squad, their empties cashed
for good,
With dauntless mien, but complexion green, Cuthbert
and Milligan stood.

Herr Kapitan Humm had ordered rum (last tot for the
luckless two)
When a shout of 'Our prize' made him blink his eyes, as
Bagpipe hove in view.
Cuthbert and Milligan finished their rum, then swooned
with a cook-like thud,
As tied to the side of the pride of Clyde, they spied the
Christmas pud.

He raised the duff with a Heilan's screech (and that is
hard to beat)
'Der giant mine—Der dumpkof schwein!' Herr Kapitan
cried, 'Retreat!'
Over the dunes and far away (good time was made in the
rough)
With Humm at their head, the Fritzes fled, from
Bagpipe's Christmas duff.

Bunting gay on Il Muzzo way and the Colonel's happy
tears
As the soldiers stood to greet the pud and YMCA stood
beers,
Gaily alight with blazing meth—which we aver is the
stuff,
While the brass band played Schubert's Serenade, the
cooks bore up the duff.

Loud may Haw-Haw jeer and rage, Britain will keep the seas,
And the Empire Fair need not despair, while we have men like these,
In thirty or forty years from now, when the Blitzkrieg rages rough,
Let us tell in the sand of this desert land, the tale of the Christmas duff.

Pte. F. St Bruno

4

Wartime Experiences

From the point of view of the welfare of English literature, one of the curses of having a war was the numbers of elegant young men from the home counties who became 2nd lieutenants and, daydreaming of being proclaimed the Rupert Brooke of World War II, churned out yards of pretentious, florid verse describing their attitudes towards suffering, death and the like.

Worse still, they submitted their high-faluting drivel to London publishers who gathered it together and, squandering scarce stocks of paper that could have been usefully allocated to printing more Hank Jansons, put out anthologies under such silly titles as *Flowers from the Western Desert.* Civilians then bought them under the delusion that it was a patriotic act to do so.

Fortunately, these Milton Milkweeds of the officers' messes were not the only members of the armed forces to turn to poetry as a means of expressing what they felt about their experiences. Some conscripted privates, alumni of council schools whose training in poesy had been restricted to reading the insides of Woolworth's greeting cards and rewriting hymns to give them dirty meanings, produced verses that were fresh, spirited and convincing. Technically, much of what they wrote was doggerel, but what of it?

It was, of course, these worthwhile, however crude, pieces that never saw the light of day.

To my mind, the best of those that I have received is *A Night in Germany—1944*, the second in this section. Its chances of being admitted to the *Oxford Book of Modern Verse* are somewhat slim. Yet it conveys, as more polished poems lamentably fail to do, what it was like to be there, which is surely the point.

Troopship to Malta

By the northern deep sea waters
Where the seas are deep and green,
There at anchor in safe harbour
Many goodly ships were seen.

From the north and from the eastward,
From the south and from the west,
Came the troops of Merrie England
All dressed in their Sunday best.

Little topees slung behind them,
Badges gleaming, kitbags clean,
Such a motley crowd of fellows
That Britain's shores had ever seen.

Here come sturdy men of Hampshire,
Stalwart sailors by the score,
Well-bronzed men from sunny Dorset,
To the troopship off the shore.

Some were happy, some were sullen.
Some were moody, others gay,
Brought by tender to the troopship,
Pouring into her all day.

Below you heard their many voices,
Southern drawl or midland twang,
A voice of many a western city,
Or a cockney who didn't care a damn.

Now the convoy steams about us,
Warships herd us into line,
Leaving England's shores behind us,
And our loved ones, yours and mine.

We found ourselves installed in quarters,
Bunks awaiting, row on row,
Sorting out our new equipment,
Wondering where we had to go.

Is it Gib, or is it Malta,
Africa or Cyprus fair?
We ask the sailor men around us,
Could they lay the secret bare?

But all is hush-hush, there's no knowing,
If it's Iceland or fair Capri,
Being merely private soldiers,
We can only wait and see.

It's just a question now of waiting,
Or lining up for dry canteen,
Just sleeping, eating, hoping, praying,
That land ahead will soon be seen.

Came the day, long last we saw you,
All the journey battled through,
The age old fortress isle of Malta,
Rising there from out the blue.

From the rail we stood and scanned you,
Watchdog, standing firm and fast.
Soon to share your common danger,
Malta was relieved at last.

A Night in Germany - 1944

Outside the moon is riding high
As tanks along the road go by,
But here inside with the aid of a lamp
A bloke on a melodeon tries to vamp.

The cellar is low and dark as well,
How so many sleep there is hard to tell.
We sit all over the floor so hard
Awaiting our turn to go out on guard.

Then out we go, overcoat and tin hat,
For out in the trench you are bound to need that.
As you stand and look in the darkness ahead
Into No-Man's Land where all seems dead.

Then the silence is broken by the sound of a shell
From out of the distance it whistles like hell.
Then the whistle gets louder. You pull your head in.
The shell comes to earth with a hell of a din.

You say to your mate, 'That bugger was near,'
To which he replies, 'There's another one here.'
Again you get your head nearer the ground
And over again wait for that horrible sound.

Away to the right and over the hill
Machine guns are chattering, loud and shrill,
Whilst away to the left round the bend of the road
The twenty-five-pounders deliver a load.

After a while the noise dies away
But things in Germany are still not so gay,
For in the distance their sirens we hear.
This gladly denotes that the RAF's here.

In a matter of minutes with a deafening roar
The four-engined monsters go flying o'er.
The searchlights go up to hunt the dark sky
But the lads in the planes keep them up far too high.

Once again it is quiet and everything's still,
No noise up the road or over the hill.
Once again we resume our vigilant stare,
As we look for something we hope is not there.

What's that that made the damned wire rattle?
It may be the Hun, it may be the cattle.
We look and we listen. I feel my skin creep.
Then a flare goes up. Whew! It's one of those sheep.

'Halt!' cries my mate as footsteps come near,
Just loud enough for the person to hear.
'Guard commander,' the call comes, we sigh a deep sigh.
'Thank God' says my mate. 'Let's get some shut-eye.'

Then back in the cellars where the fire burns bright
Bill lies on his bed and I try to write
A few lines to the wife, whose presence I miss,
Specially after a night like this.

So war goes on and day follows night,
And we go on fighting for a cause that is right—
For King and country and those we hold dear,
And hope that we never again shall come here.

The Bar-Room Cads

Practical jokes and ragging helped combat the tedium of army life.

'Allah H. Buksh' writes:

'Frequent in Catterick in early service days was to be woken up by bods coming in from a night on the town, usually under the influence of too many NAAFI buns. They would wake up someone who was soundly sleeping and inquire whether the sleeper wished to buy either a battleship or a bren-gun carrier. If you were of the hardier type, you would bide your time and then, when the rowdy ones were well asleep, wake them in return and ask 'How much?'

'At Ripon transit camp, which was a former prisoner-of-war camp, the WC cubicles were placed over a common long trough which carted away the spoil by means of a constant flow of water along the trough. The wags would wait until the chosen victim was well settled on a seat, perhaps to while away ten minutes with a Hank Janson (much sought after then): they would then float a large ball of burning newspaper along the water trough, giving the leisurely reader a thoroughly warmed-up derriere.'

But sometimes the jokes could turn very sour indeed.

'Twas the witching hour of midnight
All the bar-room cads were there,
Around one cabin on C deck
Hung a silent, sinister air.

They opened wide the portal,
Dived into that cabin dark,
Where a recumbent form was lying
'Twas that of the soldier's nark.

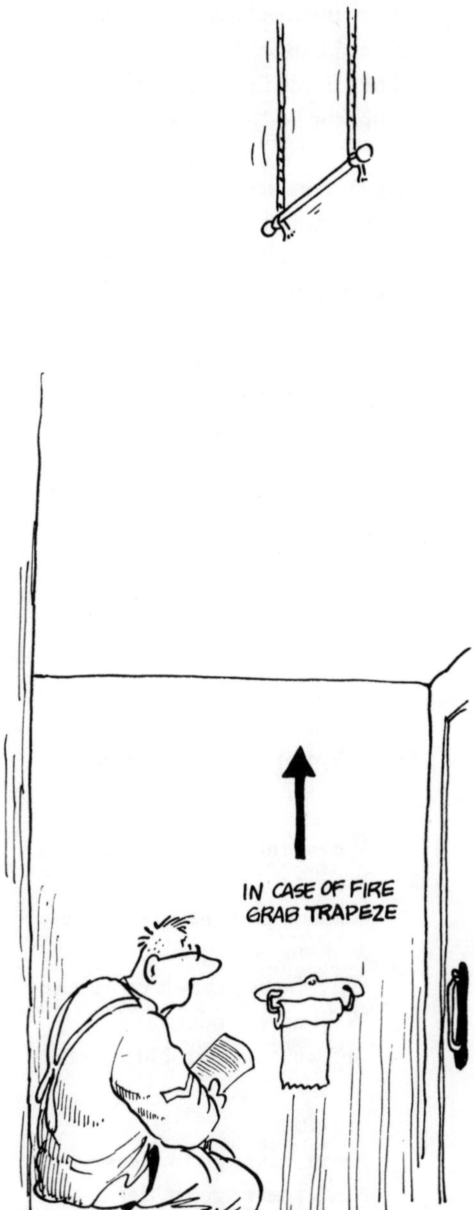
IN CASE OF FIRE
GRAB TRAPEZE

They pounced upon the carcass,
Placed a towel upon its head,
Then in the inky darkness,
Tore the body off the bed.

The victim screamed for mercy,
Face covered with foam and spit.
Said one to the other with eyes full of dread:
'The bugger's thrown a fit.'

The moral to this story,
When the bar-room cads get tight:
Is away with honour and glory
And lock your doors at night.

Never go to Mersa

We eat the flies, we eat the shit,
We eat the burning sand.
Our bones are getting brittle
And our faces getting tanned.
Why the hell they keep us here
We'll never understand,
But we'll sing our blues away.

CHORUS
Never, never go to Mersa
Never, never go to Mersa
Never, never go to Mersa
It's a lousy place to stay.

Every Sunday morning,
We march across the sand.
The padre stands before us
With his Bible in his hand.
We give our thanks to God
And join his happy band,
As we sing our blues away.

CHORUS

In Italy, 1944

The eighty-eights they whistle by
And Spandaus chill our blood;
We're thankful for our slitties
As we lie here in the mud.
The great guns roar and thunder
And smoke clouds fill the sky,
While up on top our shufti planes
Tell us where Jerries lie.
Our water bottle's had it
(What's known as 'out the monk')—
We'll have to eat our biscuits dry
Without the usual dunk.
Now all you would-be soldiers,
Just take advice from me—
If you want to live to a ripe old age
Then join the ASC.*

* Army Service Corps.

Riposte

'Then join the ASC,' he says;
But little does he think
Of the service they have rendered
In every show or stink.
Of course we get around a bit,
'Twixt Rome and dump and front,
But everything's not roses
When trucks are out the monk.

It's not all fun just sitting there
With ammo on the back
When bombs are dropping all around
And skies are full of flack.
We're frequently up front, you know—
Not always in the rear;
The Arty want their ammo,
And get it, never fear.

With eighty-eights and mortars
We sometimes have to deal.
We can't crouch in a slittie
While swinging on a wheel.
The PBI can take it—
You've often heard it said:
But we're the boys who BRING it—
Just get that in your head.

Why?

I often think, dear God why,
Did all those men go out to die?
Their blood soaked up into the sand,
Fighting in a foreign land.

In my thoughts I see them still,
Snowy, Taffy, Knocker, Bill,
Jack Cowie and Jock Sutherland,
And all my other mates so grand.

The East

We have all heard of golden sands
And wish to see those far-off lands,
To look around the deserts and roam.
Now my advice is: stay at home.
Those tales of love beneath the stars
May pass an hour away.
But love back home, yes in a fog,
Is better any day.
These tales don't tell of things that are
Of natives, you can smell them from afar,
Who clamber round and ask baksheesh,
All of them with different pleas,
Of sheep and goats, with scabs all over,
Sleep with kiddies on the floor,
Of disease they never tell,
The kind that makes this life a hell,
Human bodies bought so cheap,
They never tell of Burka Street.

Christmas in Cairo

Me Christmas spirit's burning dim and me Christmas cheque is slim,
I've seen the Yuletides good and bad, but never one so grim,
So jack me up a bottle, dig, and hear my tale of woe,
How I'm the sole remaining one of the gang I used to know.

You find me lonesome in a Naafi drinking to my sins,
Sipping like a Jimmy Woodser: and here's the yarn I spins:
Of Platoon Number Three of Company C, the mob I trained among.
The last of a band that hit this land when the Sphinx was only young.

That mob, they stuck together tight while training for the fight
And fought like hell to the final bell, when the blitz was at its height;
Then back at base they set the pace, when bludging was an art
But some are dead and some are gone and drinking's lost its heart.

So now that gang has gone to hang, and days of yore are through.
I hear that Ollie's up at OCTU* and Dusty's in the Blue.
The sun got Slim and finished him as far as fighting goes.
He asks for rum and they hand him milk and he never even knows.

---

* Officer Cadets Training Unit.

Then Butch is in the carocol, what comes of drinking
alcohol,
He picks a fight, most impolite, with a guy about a doll;
Well Butch says he's winning, and I guess mebbe is at
that,
But if you please, the red he sees is on the fella's hat.

Old Bert, the cow with the luck of a Chow, has gone
home APR
He left a note in which he wrote: 'Saieeda, George,
Hurrah,'
But never a line, a word or sign to soften the bitter blow
Of losing the quid I'd kindly lent a year and more ago.

Then Blue's along of Butch a-lugging boulders small and
large,
'Twas C to the P of M and D*, or some such horrid
charge.
They sent old Bill to Bludger's Hill, and jacked him up a
stripe
He now wears socks and cleans his teeth and even
learned to type.

And Rommel's wallahs collected Hank for trying to
pinch a ruddy tank.
Me old man's in the EPS: me girl has met a Yank:
From letters I've had, the blackout's bad, and things at
home are tough
The tea is weak, and so's the beer, from Auckland to the
Bluff.

---

* Conduct to the Prejudice of Military Discipline.

Well, I ask you pal, now what the hell it's worth to look
ahead
Me paybook's sadly overdrawn, there's bed-bugs in me
bed.
So here's a toast to the Yuletide ghost, and the mob
when times were good.
I wish to state, so help me mate—it certainly flaming
well would.

J.S.H.

A Soldier. His Prayer

This poem is different from the others in that it was written by a well-known writer and that it was published many times during the 1940s. I include it here partly because the bizarre story behind it has been known only to a very small circle of people.

Its author was the late Gerald Kersh, whose own story is implausible enough: a Jew from the East End, he was commissioned into the Coldstream Guards and, while a guards officer, used to contribute to that rip-roaring, mass-circulation Sunday newspaper, *The People*.

Kersh, I am told, scribbled off *A Soldier. His Prayer* rather quickly, sent it to *The People*, which published it, and thought little more about it until sometime later.

Then his poem was reprinted in a book of forces' verse. Instead of being attributed to him, an introductory note claimed that the author was unknown, and that it had come to light when a soldier in a dug-out in the desert saw a scrap of paper wafting towards him in the breeze over the sand dunes. When it reached him, he picked it up out of idle curiosity, read it, and, deeply moved, passed it around his mates. In his introduction to the collection, Field-Marshal Montgomery expressed himself as having been specially moved by *A Soldier. His Prayer*, and dwelt upon the almost mystical circumstances of its discovery.

This fable about its origins, together with Monty's imprimatur, produced an electric response. It became by far the most popularly acclaimed poem to come out of the war. Mothers copied it out and sent it to their sons in the services. Clergymen read it to their congregations. Elderly ladies embroidered it on to samplers. A best-selling record was produced, on which it was declaimed over a background of solemn music.

Less edifyingly, when Kersh self-effacingly refused to come forward and identify himself as the man who had written it, there was a wild rush of people claiming authorship either on behalf of themselves or of a relative—usually a son—who had been killed in action and, allegedly, sent it home in a letter just before he died. Needless to say, these claims were accompanied by demands for payment for the copyright usage.

While he wanted nothing from it for himself, these shameless and fraudulent bids to cash in did annoy Kersh exceedingly. Perhaps the one that annoyed him most was one from Australia, because it was lodged by a clergymen and he expected men of the cloth to behave themselves with greater moral rectitude. By chance, Kersh's brother Cyril, now a senior executive on the *Sunday Mirror*, was serving in Australia in the Navy: and Gerald asked him to call on the clergyman.

Cyril did so, without making a prior appointment, during the course of a weekend leave. He says that the clergyman concerned opened the front door himself, but the moment he learned his caller's surname, slammed it again and would not reappear.

In Cairo, the poem was the subject of a better intentioned fraud. A small group of officers claimed that it had first come to light when it was found, tattered and blood-stained on a scrap of paper, in the pocket next to the heart of a Desert Rat who had died a hero's death. Having faked this 'original', they auctioned it off for a large sum, for the benefit of the Red Cross.

Stay with me, God. The night is dark.
The night is cold. My little spark
Of courage dies. The night is long;
Be with me, God, and make me strong.

I love a game; I love a fight.
I hate the dark; I love the light.
I love my child; I love my wife;
I am no coward; I love life.

Life with its change of mood and shade;
I want to live. I'm not afraid,
But me and mine are hard to part.
Oh unknown God, lift up my heart.

You stilled the waters at Dunkirk
And saved your servants. All your work
Is wonderful, dear God; You strode
Before us down that dreadful road.

We were alone, and hope had fled.
We loved our country and our dead
And could not shame them; so we stayed
The course, and were not much afraid.

Dear God, that nightmare road! And then
That sea! We got there—we were men.
My eyes were blind, my feet were torn.
My soul sang like a bird at dawn.

I know that Death is but a door.
I knew what we were fighting for;
Peace for the kids, our brothers freed,
A kinder world, a cleaner breed.

I'm but the son my mother bore,
A simple man and nothing more.
But God of strength and gentleness,
Be pleased to make me nothing less.

Help me, God, when death is near,
To mock the haggard face of fear
That when I fall, if fall I must,
My soul may triumph in the dust.

The Fuzzy-Wuzzy Angels

In the fight against the Japanese in New Guinea, many an Australian who had previously regarded 'abos' with something like contempt, discovered a new-found respect for the New Guineans.

Stretcher-parties made up of volunteer 'fuzzy-wuzzies', as they were called—at first patronisingly and then affectionately—showed great bravery in going into the fighting areas to retrieve the wounded, and won great gratitude for the gentleness they combined with great powers of endurance.

The Fuzzy-Wuzzy Angels was composed by an unknown Australian in their honour, and it became an extremely popular recitation among the Australian troops.

Many a mother in Australia, when the busy day is done,
Sends a prayer to the Almighty, for the keeping of her son;
Asking that an angel guide him and bring him safely back—
Now we see those prayers are answered on the Owen Stanley Track.
Though they haven't any haloes, only holes slashed through the ear,
And their faces marked with tattoos and with scratchpins in their hair,
Bringing back the badly wounded, just as steady as a hearse,
Using leaves to keep the rain off, and as gentle as a nurse;
Slow and careful in bad places, on the awful mountain track,
And the look upon their faces makes us think that Christ was black.
Not a move to hurt the carried, as they treat him like a saint,
It's a picture worth recording that an artist's yet to paint.
Many a lad will see his mother, and the husbands, wee'uns and wives
Just because the fuzzy-wuzzies carried them to save their lives.
From mortar or machine-gun fire or a chance surprise attack
To safety and care of doctors at the bottom of the track
May the mothers in Australia, when they offer up a prayer
Mention these impromptu angels with the fuzzy-wuzzy hair.

5

The Gremlins in the Sky

OLD IRON
'You know what you can do
With your Barracuda II,
Old iron, old iron!'

The story was told of the man who was desperately keen to join the Air Force, but kept failing the intelligence tests. Eventually they took pity on him and told him he could become a rear-gunner for four shillings a day pay.

'How much is that a week?' he asked dumbly.

'We don't know,' the recruiting officer replied. 'We haven't had one yet who lasted that long.'

It is a striking aspect of conscripts' reactions to being in the war that few were exposed to greater danger than the air-crews, yet probably nowhere in the armed forces was morale higher.

And the risk of being shot at by the Germans was only part of the danger. It is said that more men died on account of poor equipment, mechanical failure and pilot error than from enemy action.

'Gremlins' was the name given to the mythical, macabrely funny beasts in the sky who were blamed for the things that repeatedly and sometimes fatally kept going wrong during missions.

The origin is normally attributed to an unknown pilot drinking—drinking too much—with some colleagues in a pub near an airfield in the wilds of East Anglia. Fremlins is a local beer and, muddling his words, he said: 'Frab me a Gremlin, please, old boy.' The name seemed just right, and it stuck.

Unidentified Objects

To the tune of 'The Eton Boating Song'

This is the tale of the Gremlins
Told by the PRU*
At Benson and Wick and St Eval—
And believe me, you slobs, it is true.

* Photographic Reconnaissance Unit.

When you're seven miles up in the heavens,
(That's a hell of a lonely spot)
And it's fifty degrees below zero
Which isn't exactly hot.

When you're frozen blue like your Spitfire
And you're scared a Mosquito pink,
When you're thousands of miles from nowhere
And there's nothing below but the drink—

It's then you will see the Gremlins,
Green and gamboge and gold,
Male and female and neuter,
Gremlins both young and old.

It's no good trying to dodge them.
The lessons you learned on the Link
Won't help you evade a Gremlin
Though you boost and you dive and you jink.

White ones will wiggle your wingtips,
Male ones will muddle your maps
Green ones will guzzle your Glycol,
Females will flutter your flaps.

Pink ones will perch on your perspex,
And dance pirouettes on your prop;
There's a spherical middle-aged Gremlin
Who'll spin on your stick like a top.

They'll freeze up your camera shutters,
They'll bite through your aileron wires.
They'll bend and they'll break and they'll batter,
They'll insert toasting forks in your tyres.

That is the tale of the Gremlins
Told by the PRU,
Pretty Ruddy Unlikely to many,
But fact, none the less, to the few.

Barracuda II

Perhaps no group of fighting men was more terrified of their own equipment than the pilots who flew Barracuda IIs from the flight decks of aircraft carriers.

Clumsy and outmoded, they were inordinately hard to handle, unreliable and fell from the sky with the greatest of ease.

Looking back, it is almost surprising that the men were willing to fly them at all, despite the demands of military discipline. But, as one after another crashed, those pilots who remained, instead of openly rebelling, sang songs like these before they took off.

Fairey, a name reviled in these songs was, of course, the plane's manufacturer.

Old Iron

Any old iron! Any old iron! Any any any old iron!
Talk about a treat,
Torpedoing a fleet,
Any old cruiser or battleship you meet.
Weighs six tons, no front guns,
Fuck all to rely on.
You know what you can do
With your Barracuda II,
Old iron, old iron!

Any old iron! Any old iron! Any any any old iron!
The engine is a teased Rolls Royce—
A Merlin 32, and it ain't our choice.
Open up the throttle
And the whole fucking lot'll
Wail like an air-raid siren.
You know what you can do
With your Barracuda II,
Old iron, old iron!

Such a Fucking Crate

To the tune of 'As Time Goes By'

It's called the Barracuda
And nothing could be cruder
Still flying in the sky.
You really can't believe it's true
As one goes by.

Observer and air-gunner
Weigh down this seven-tonner,
And they will tell you why
They're happy to be on the ground
As one goes by.

High-strutted tailplane very out of date,
Radar and wireless adding to the weight,
High wing and dive brakes—such a fucking crate
Could never really fly.

That two-ton pair of legs
Is just the bloody dregs—
That Fairey's can't deny.
The RAF just rub their eyes
As one goes by.

Fairey! Fairey!

To the tune of 'Daisy, Daisy'

Fairey! Fairey! Give me your answer do,
What is wrong with my Barracuda II?
Dive-bombing has strained my structure,
I've got a stressed-skin rupture,
And rivets pop
Along the top
And one of them might hit you.

Fairey! Fairey! What are we going to do?
Nine Wing's grounded—looks pretty bad for you.
When my Barra falls as under
I'll be a wingless wonder
I'll jump out quick
And bring my stick
And stuff it right up you.

Thanks for the Memory!

Thanks for the memory
Of biplanes in the sky,
Of pilots who can't fly,
Of four hour trips,
Torpedoed ships,
Returning with a sigh.
How lovely it was.

CHORUS

Many's the times that we've pranged them
On many an ALT*,
And many's the times that we've slanged them
No ASV†—no W/T.‡

And thanks for the memory
Of drunken nights ashore,
Of blacks put up galore.
Of gin and limes
And flying times
And popsies by the score.
How lovely it was.

CHORUS

And thanks for the memory
Of large fixed undercarts,
Of buggers playing darts
Of Wrens galore
When we're ashore
And stormy gunners' farts.
How lovely it was.

CHORUS

---

* Altitude.
† Air-to-Surface Vision.
‡ Wireless Transmitter.

330th Squadron Song

To the tune of 'Waltzing Matilda'

Seven seedy bomber types came along to Saxonby
Posted to Squadron Three-Thirty.
And they mournfully sang
As they squelched around the nissen huts,
This is the squadron, the squadron for me.

CHORUS
Ops with three-thirty,
Ops with three-thirty,
Who'll come on ops with three-thirty and me,
And they murmured the chant as they went to see the adjutants,
Who'll come on ops with three-thirty and me.

They pressed on regardless, clueless, to Königsberg,
No defences there chaps—should be fun—
Were three hundred searchlights—never stopped to number them.
Pissed off to sea like a shot from a gun.

CHORUS

They went for a factory, a big ball-bearing factory,
Down by the shores of Lake Annecy,
And they sang as they swang and pranged it on the factory,
Balls to the bearings at Lake Annecy.

CHORUS

37th Squadron Song

We are the heavy bombers, we try to do our bit,
We fly through concentrations of flak and cloud and shit,
And when we drop our cargoes, we do not give a damn,
The goods may miss the goods yard, but they fuck up
poor old Hamm.

And when in adverse weather, the winds are all to hell,
The navigator's ballsed up, the wireless ballsed as well,
We think of all the popsies we've known in days gone by
And curse the silly fuckers who taught us how to fly.

They sent us out to Egypt, a very pleasant land,
Where miles and miles of sweet fuck-all are covered up
in sand,
And when we got to Cairo, the girls were heard to say,
'There ain't no hope for us, dears, thirty-seventh's come
to stay!'

And when you get to Hades, it's just like SHQ,
With lots of stooges sitting around with fuck-all else to
do.
They ask you for your flimsies, your target maps and
pass.
You take the ruddy issue and stick it up their arse.

6

Love, Lust and the Like

She loves you, trusts you, breathes in prayer your name;
Soil not her faith in you, by sin or shame.

So wrote the home-front poetess Margaret Scruton in her tremulous verse-plea to men who had been called away to fight, to resist base sexual temptations while they were far from home, and to return to their loved ones glowing with chastity.

Mrs Scruton's *For Honour, and For Her!* with which this section begins, was a popular work among women, and even some men who like that kind of thing, and it conjured up a poignant picture of the lone wife waiting by the fireside, brimming with noble love, unwavering in her fidelity and infinite in her silent fortitude, while her absent husband went on randy rampages.

Poignant it may have been and, in its way, well-intentioned too. But it was also, whether or not Mrs Scruton knew it, a tasteless and insensitive distortion of the reality of the situation. While the great majority of women did remain faithful to their menfolk away fighting, it was also the case that during the war, when infidelities of the kind that break up marriages occurred, almost every time it was the wives who committed them.

Contrary to civilian myth, even now being bolstered by such books as Leslie Thomas's best-selling *Virgin Soldiers*, not many men used call-up as a launching pad for sexual adventure. Of course they said otherwise when boasting in the pub on home leave—to have done otherwise would have damaged their *machismo*. But for all the barrack-room bragging, the bandying about in the billets of appalling sexual advice (e.g. 'When yer gets 'er into the pictures, just whip it out and put 'er 'and on it') and the free army issue of condoms (known as 'sports gear'), the padres' sermons about resisting temptations of the flesh left most of them wondering where they were thought to be finding it.

In England, soldiers' pay, particularly after most of it had been remitted home, did not stretch to nights out with girls. Abroad, it was true, there were brothels catering to servicemen. But as I was able to discover for myself when a war correspondent, it normally took a serviceman of quite exceptional lack of discrimination and really consuming frustration to repeat the experience of using one. And probably the majority never did. Every serviceman in Cairo knew of the legendary tart, Tiger Lil. She was the one prostitute who offered her customers satisfaction, and, of course, she never existed.

Later, in South-east Asia, British servicemen used to crowd into bars frequented by loose women. But my observation was that they rarely retired upstairs to consummate a deal—they went, in many cases, for a bit of feminine company and seemed to crave mothering more than sex.

The women in the forces were virtually taboo, to the extent that some of them used to delight in taunting new recruits, making them blush and flee, by chanting in unison: 'How about a fuck?' The taboo was not universally honoured—at least one unfortunate girl left the WRACs with a note pinned to her back by her friends: 'Return When Empty'—but such incidents were comparatively rare.

It is, in fact, a remarkable but little remarked upon phenomenon of call-up that it frequently induced in its victims an immediate and lasting impotence. This was the foundation for the rumour, believed by countless other ranks, that the authorities had bromide put in the forces' tea to quell their lust. To have admitted that the real reasons for their loss of interest in sex were insufficient surplus energy, the—to say the least—unerotic environment, and fear, would have been unthinkable. So the obvious thing was to blame it on the Government.

In their free time servicemen were prone to gravitate towards beer rather than to wanton girls. Their preoccupation with the fermented grain and hop in the face of all counter-attractions was the basis of many jokes, such as this.

A shipwrecked sailor floated on a life-raft in the Atlantic for many days before he was picked up by a lifeboat from the shore. Taken to the nearest harbour, he was greeted by a civilian committee of welcome, which included the town's beauty queen. She ceremonially kissed him, then whispered in his ear, 'When this is over, I'm going to take you to my flat and give you something you haven't had in a long, long time.'

'My God,' he replied. 'You don't mean to say that you've got a bottle of beer?'

It was some of the wives left at home who had the days of leisure, the double bed and the inclination to stray from the matrimonial straight and narrow. And as is notorious, even if the milkman had been called to arms, there was no shortage of members of the opposite sex at their disposal, in the form of American, Canadian, French, Polish and other allied servicemen. The amount of adultery that went on in England was an unreported scandal of the war years.

The Germans sought to exploit it by mounting a black propaganda campaign by means of which selected British servicemen in the Middle East received anonymous letters, correctly addressed with rank and number, bearing the message: 'A CANADIAN SOLDIER THANKS YOU FOR THE SERVICES OF YOUR WIFE.'

It was in its way a shrewdly conceived and efficiently executed exercise in the demoralisation of one's enemy, except for one mistake—Dr Goebbels's minions kept sending the letters to men who weren't married.

The Germans' painstaking initiative was, in any case, probably superfluous. Their work was being done for them by

the British wives themselves. A bitter 8th Army anecdote told of the man who received a letter from his wife saying she wanted a divorce because she had fallen in love with a GI. 'What's he got that I haven't?' he wrote back. 'Nothing,' she replied, 'but he's got it here.'

One of the verses that follows is angry in its protest against the long delays the men experienced in receiving mail from home. But for some of those in North Africa it was a moot point which they feared the most—their imaginings as to what was going on back home in the absence of any news, or the prospect of receiving a letter confirming their worries.

'Dear Johns' flowed remorselessly from England to the Western Desert. By the middle of the war, so many women were writing to ask for their freedom so that they could marry a foreigner that both the Army and the RAF found it necessary to set up teams of solicitors in the desert to help process the divorces from the war-fronts.

One of these lawyers, Squadron-Leader E. B. Wight, who himself married while in the Mediterranean war zone a forces' social worker, has kindly given me the items that appear in the section entitled *Dear John*.

'Her kiss, her words, will cheer you in the strife,' declared Mrs Scruton. It didn't seem that way to the men in the queues outside the solicitors' tents in Mersa Matruh.

For Honour and for Her!

Somewhere a woman, thrusting fear away,
Faces the future bravely for your sake;
Toils on from dawn to dark; from day to day;
Fights back her tears, nor heeds the bitter ache;
She loves you, trusts you, breathes in prayer your name;
Soil not her faith in you, by sin or shame.

Somewhere a woman—mother, sweetheart, wife—
Waits betwixt hopes and fears, for your return;
Her kiss, her words, will cheer you in the strife,
When death itself confronts you, grim and stern;
But let her image all reverence claim,
When base temptations scorch you with their flame.

Somewhere a woman watches, filled with pride;
Shrined in her heart, you share a place with none;
She toils, she waits, she prays, till side by side
You stand together when the battle's done.
O keep for her dear sake a stainless name.
Bring back to her a manhood free from shame!

Margaret Scruton

Stella!

'Twas coming from Gazala that
We came across a Desert Rat.
'Oh bring me Stella!' we heard him cry,
'I must have Stella before I die.'

We conjured up a mirage there
Of English womanhood so fair
Of Stella, so far away, who sat
And wept for that dying Desert Rat.

But we were wrong, we were to find.
His thoughts were of a different kind.
It was no woman he held so dear,
But his favourite brand of Cairo beer.

The Fucking Mail Run

To the tune of 'Clementine'

Down the flights each fucking morning
Sitting waiting for a clue
Some old notice on the Flights Board:
'Maximum effort—guess where to?'

CHORUS

Seventy squadron, seventy squadron,
Though we say it with a sigh,
We must do the fucking mail run
Every day until we die.

'Have you lost us, navigator?
Come up here and take a look—
Someone's shot our starboard wing off.
We're all right then, that's Tobruk.'

CHORUS

Oh to be in Piccadilly
Selling matches by the score.
Then we should not have to do the
Fucking mail run any more.

CHORUS

Censorship

When Mrs Malone got a letter from Pat
She started to read it aloud in her flat.
'Dear Mary,' it started, 'If you have a map,
I'm somewhere in . . . and I'm fighting the . . .
I'm choking with news I'd like to relate
But it's little a soldier's permitted to state.
Do ye mind Red McPhee? Well he fell in a ditch
And busted his arm, but I can't tell you which,
And Paddy O'Hara was caught in a flame.
He was rescued by . . . Faith, I can't tell you the name.
Last night I woke up wid a terrible pain.
I thought for a while it would drive me insane.
Oh the suffering I had was most dreadful to bear.
I'm sorry, my dear, but I can't tell you where.
The doctor just gave me a pill, but I find
It's contrary to rules to tell you what kind.
I have been to the dentist to have a tooth out,
I am sorry to leave you so shrouded in doubt.
But the most I can say is that one tooth is gone,
The censor won't let me inform you which one.
I met a young fellow who knows you right well,
And you know him too, but his name I can't tell.
He is Irish, red-headed and there with the blarney.
His folks knew your folks, back home in Killarney.'
'Begorrah,' said Mrs Malone in her flat,
'It's hard to make sense of writing like that.
But I'll give him as good as he sends, that I will,'
And she went right to work with her ink and her quill,
And she wrote: 'I suppose you're dead eager for news.
You know when you left you were buying the shoes.
Well, the baby has come and we're both doing well.
It's a . . . Oh, but that's something the censor won't let
me tell.'

Aunt Mathilda's Advice Corner

The identity of the serviceman who used the nom-de-plume 'Aunt Mathilda' is unknown. 'She' contributed columns of sardonic advice about love problems, published in *The Arctic Times*, for British troops in Iceland.

The following item summed up her basic message.

Dear Aunt Mathilda,

My girlfriend at home says she's browned off with living on her own and me out here and says she wants loving. So she has picked up a fresh bloke and says she's going to marry him, and do I mind, and would I please send her the sealskin gloves as promised as they will come in nice for a wedding present.

Do you think I can get compassionate leave to go home and marry her myself?

A: Well, sap, you may get home in time for the christening, if you hurry.

Dear John

The solicitors who handled British servicemen's divorces for them from the Western Desert and later Italy, spent day after day being shown letters from wives back home, asking for their freedom.

Eventually, one lunchtime, they composed a draft form incorporating all the clichés, with the sarcastic aim of saving the wives the trouble of writing them out for themselves.

FAIRLY CONFIDENTIAL

UFW/Preg/confess/xxx/1

PRO-FORMA FOR USE BY WIVES OF SOLDIERS SERVING OVERSEAS

(*Obtainable from all Post Offices, Labour Exchanges and Ante-natal Clinics.*)
Issued pursuant to section 69 of the UK Troops (Prohibition of Leave) and Allied Forces (Entertainments) Act, 1945.

Strike out words not applicable

Dear
Darling
Mr
My Loving Husband
I hope this finds you in the pink as it leaves me.
This will come as a great shock/terrible surprise to you but please don't do anything rash to yourself/I wouldn't do.

I do not know how to tell you/say it.

I have had a baby/have fallen for a child/am in trouble (again).

I met a Canadian/American/Dutchman/Pole/Free Frenchman/Greek/Italian Prisoner who was cheeky/a nasty bugger/a nice boy/a dirty old man.

We only had a few/had a good many drinks at .... and I don't know/of course you can guess what happened.

He forced me/It all happened so quickly/slowly. I did/did not like it.

It only happened once/twice/ . . . times.

Please forgive me/I don't suppose you'll forgive me.

Please divorce me/give me my freedom/give me another chance.

I love him/you.

You know I was always/never in love with you.

I will/will not have it adopted/put away.

Your broken-hearted/loving/ever-loving/lonely/faithful wife,

Mrs . . . . . .

(insert Xs to taste.)

PS It was on the common/in the kitchen/in the dark.

Middle Eastern Law Notes

Scene: A very dirty city somewhere in the Mediterranean.

Solicitor	(*in uniform*) Yes.
Private Swaddie	It's the wife.
Solicitor	Yes.
Swaddie	She wants a divorce—see.
Solicitor	You mean she wants to divorce you?
Swaddie	She wants one, see, and I said I'd give it her.
Solicitor	Has she grounds against you?

Swaddie assumes a vacant look.

Solicitor You realise that divorce can only be obtained if there are grounds—have you committed adultery or deserted your wife?

Swaddie Oh no, not me.

Solicitor Has your wife committed adultery?

Swaddie I don't know. I didn't ask her. You see she wants the divorce and I said I'd give her one.

Six months later.

Solicitor Well, you now have sufficient evidence against your wife. You understand the meaning of the word adultery?

Swaddie I'm not sure that I rightly do.

Solicitor explains.

Swaddie Well, I've had a bit at odd times, like.

Solicitor How many times?

Swaddie I can't rightly remember. I've been out here a long time.

Solicitor Last time I saw you, you said you had not committed adultery.

Swaddie Well, it was in brothels mostly. I didn't think it counted.

And so on. And so on.

With characteristic barminess, the armed forces, having found themselves regretfully obliged to provide legal facilities to enable unfaithful wives to divorce their husbands serving in the war, then set itself the task of getting as many of its men divorced as possible.

Heaven may have rejoiced in last-minute reconciliations, but down here on earth they played havoc with the military lawyers' productivity ratings. The authorities compiled and distributed a monthly league table as a means of commending those officers with the highest scores of couples put asunder.

Squadron-Leader Wight was moved to protest as follows.

Confidential

In this race for memoranda it is manifestly plain
That the laurels for this month of March are due to
Major Lane
Are we to infer from this mere quickness of the wrist?
Or is it merely sleight of hand that makes him head
the list?

At the Florence Forward Section where Wight and
Winston toil
Their exists a friendly rivalry, their clients to embroil
In Divorce and Separation: and thus the figures
mount.
Alas! the man has too much means; I wonder, will
this count?

There are few things more depressing where adultery can be shown
To find the wife is writing letters most affectionate in tone.
'I know the little bastard's black, but please, forgive me do!'
And the Client shows a preference for the woman's point of view.

Oh! It's galling and degrading when the figures are compiled,
To find from eighty interviews that half are reconciled.
Persuasion, oratory are vain; the men won't bow to reason.
He loves the bitch! No memo! Damn, is this the mating season?

From henceforth we shall emulate the standard set by Ralph;
We will warn them that forgiveness is a plan that isn't safe.
We must produce more memos just to keep the figures rising,
And if London find they can't cope—well, that's really not surprising.

Divorce Lawyer's Limerick

James Denning, a lawyer at Bone,
To the law section added some tone.
His advice on divorces
To all in the Forces
Was collude, then connive, then condone.

Why not forget it?

Do you remember the night that we met,
In that glorious vale by the sea?
Such marvellous things I told you my pet,
As you lovingly nestled to me.
Could you ever forget our last, long embrace?
Were you sad I was sailing away?
And did I not promise a comfortable place
After a wedding some day?
I hope you remember, I really don't know—
Our party that night had been wet—
So tell me—just how far did I go?
Well now I hope you'll forget.

My Love has a Pip on her Shoulder

We were young, we were gay, we were lovers,
And the world was a garden of flowers;
Now the blossoms are faded and fallen
And a winter unending is ours.
We are parted and parted for ever,
Condemned beyond hope of reprieve,
For my love has a pip on her shoulder
And I but a stripe on my sleeve.

We have met since it happened, but somehow
Proud Lance Bombardier though I am,
I cannot make love at attention
While addressing my loved one as 'ma'am'.

I cannot make love at attention
While addressing my loved one as 'ma'am'.

Oh the spirit of Anzac assist me,
A soldier has no right to grieve,
But my love had a pip on her shoulder
And I but a stripe on my sleeve.

So play me *Flowers of the Forest*
Let me drain sorrow's cup to the dregs.
I have loved as a carefree civilian,
I have lost as laid down in King's Regs.
Let me burnish the breech of my Bofors,
And forget about seven days' leave.
For my love had a pip on her shoulder
And I but a stripe on my sleeve.

Aden

It was in a Maala backstreet,
Standing by the brothel door
Stood a tall and proud young airman
Equipped to go to war.

And standing there beside him,
Just before he went away
The binta leered up at him
As if she'd like to say:

'You're standing like your dad
Twenty-five years ago.
You're standing on the same doorstep
And like him you've fallen low.

'I gave him syph and gonorrhoea
And he marched from here surprised.
But he gave me plenty baksheesh
And a damned good fuck besides.

'You're just like your dad
Twenty-five years ago,
You're fighting for your country
And for all the things we know.

'You're fighting for the squalor
And all vices without name,
And if I've got to lose you
There'll be others just the same.

'No matter where you get to,
What may happen over there,
You're mauling all we bintas,
Like your father getting his share.

'To degrade the folk that love you
And destroy all they hold dear,
And whatever you may therefore gain
You'll be paying for it here.

'You're just like your dad
Twenty-five years ago,
You're fighting for your country
And all the things we know.

'You're fighting for your genitals
And lecheries—no shame—
And if we've got to lose you
I'll say *maalish* just the same.'

I'm Dreaming of a White Mistress

I'm dreaming of a white mistress,
Just like the ones we used to know.
There's no doubt about her, we can't do without her,
And she'll be white from head to toe.
On our tour of duty, many a dark skinned beauty
Has been our passing fancy quite.
But when we're at home in England at last,
Let all our mistresses be white.

7

On Ribald Ditties

It may be asked why, if so many members of the armed forces were as full of sexual inertia as I have suggested, they spent so much of their limited leisure talking and singing about sex.

The explanation is to be found in the songs themselves. They were not about sex as people know it, but of a grotesque and fantastical kind. They evoke a world in which a woman's allure is in the size of her quim, and a man's compelling attraction to members of the other sex his gigantic cock.

Such songs were in their own way bromides—it is virtually impossible to sing them and keep in one's mind what real sex is like. With all due respect to the members of the rugger clubs who keep these numbers alive, it's those who don't do it who sing them.

The Ball of Kirriemuir

This is perhaps the classic of all the military bawdy songs, and still enjoys great, if unpublicised, popularity.

Highlanders in the victory parade in Tunis, at which Winston Churchill took the salute, serenaded him with it as they marched past, to his immense amusement.

That a victorious army, fighting for democracy against a dark dictatorship, should greet its leader with a dirty song says something cheering about us, though I'm not sure what.

Alternative choruses:

1 Wha'll ha'e it noo, lads, wha'll ha'e it noo?
The yin that had it last time, ye canna ha'e it noo.

2 Balance your partner and balance to the wa',
If ye never get fucked on Saturday night, ye'll never get
fucked at a'.

First came the colonel's wife
Marching at the front,
A wreath of roses round her hair
And carrots up her cunt.

CHORUS

Then came the chaplain's wife
And she was dressed in blue.
They tied her to the barn door
And fucked her like a shoe.

CHORUS

Mrs McPherson, she was there,
She had the place in fits,
Jumping off the mantelpiece
And bouncing off her tits.

CHORUS

Then came the village postie,
He had the fucking pox.
He couldnae shag a woman
So he shagged a letter box.

CHORUS

The village idiot, he was there
And did his fav'rite trick.
He pulled his foreskin over his head
And whistled down his prick.

CHORUS

They were fucking in the bathroom,
Fucking on the stairs,
Ye couldnae see the carpet
For the stronk and curly hairs.

CHORUS

There were Campbells, there were Camerons,
McDougalls and O'Rourkes—
Ye couldnae see the barn floor
For the bottoms wanting cocks.

CHORUS

They were fucking in the courtyard,
Fucking in the ricks.
Ye couldnae hear the piper
For the swishing of the pricks.

CHORUS

So here's to guid auld Kirriemuir,
And tae its famous ball.
I cannae sing another verse,
I'm just about tae fa'.

CHORUS

No Balls at All

The night of the wedding she got into bed.
She sighed with lust, her cheeks were quite red.
She felt for his tool, and his tool was quite small.
She felt for his balls. He'd got no balls at all.
No balls, no balls at all,
She'd married a soldier with no balls at all.

She went to her mother. 'Oh mother,' she said,
'I'd rather be single. I'd rather be dead.
I don't mind a man whose got rather small balls
But balls to a soldier with no balls at all,
No balls, no balls at all,
But balls to a soldier with no balls at all.'

You can't fuck Farida if you don't pay Farouk

To the tune of the Egyptian National Anthem

Oh we're all black bastards, but we do love our king.
Every night at the flicks you can hear us fucking sing:
Quois Kettere, King Farouk!
Quois Kettere, King Farouk!
Oh you can't fuck Farida if you don't pay Farouk.

Oh we're just fucking wogs, but we do love him so,
And we all do without just to keep him on the go.
From Sollum to Sollach,
Tel-el-Kebir to Tobruk,
Oh you can't fuck Farida if you don't pay Farouk.

Oh we're just damned niggers that a bugger brought to birth,
But when we have a bint then we want our money's worth.
You may have a tarboosh,
A gamel, a gamoos,
But you can't fuck Farida if you don't pay Farouk.

Oh it's no use saying, if you want to have it in,
'Be a sport King Farouk.' He would only fucking grin.
You could beg on your knees.
He would just say 'Mafeesh'
Oh you can't get Farida if you don't pay baksheesh.

Oh his subjects all tell of the fame of King Farouk,
From Gezira to The Turf, and from Helwan to Bab-el-Louk,
They can tell what a sell
Hangs their bollocks on a hook.
For they can't fuck Farida if they don't pay Farouk.

If her boudoir you pass twixt the hours of ten and two,
You will see all the Wafdi standing waiting in a queue.
Though Nahas ain't an ass,
Though Nahas is a crook,
Still he can't fuck Farida if he don't pay Farouk.

Oh it's not hard to see poor Delilah's up a tree
For she wears the horns in the —— familee.
Old Sir Miles with his wiles
In advance tries to book.
Still he can't fuck Farida if he don't pay Farouk.

If you feel like a grind when you've had a pint of beer,
To the Berka wend your way where it ain't too fucking
dear.
Quois Kettere, Mangarihey.
Quois Kettere, Gonorrhoea.
Shufty kus. Got filoos?
Shove it up, from the rear.
For you can't fuck Farida if you don't pay Farouk.

Sung by the 1st South African Division,
9th Australian, 2nd New Zealand,
51st Highland and 7th Armoured

Dirty Gertie

Dirty Gertie from Bizerte
Hid a mouse beneath her skirts,
Made her boyfriends' fingers hurtie.
She was voted in Bizerte
Miss Latrine for 1930.

Tiger Lil

With arms akimbo, there stands Tiger Lil,
Her great big quim you'll find it hard to fill.
She'll grab your akkers, then shout out with glee;
Come all you Tank Corps queens, abide with me.

The Army Dance

To the tune of 'Come Comrades, Fill the Flowing Bowl'

First there came the general's wife,
And she was dressed in grey, sir,
And in her quite enormous quim,
She had a brewer's dray, sir.

CHORUS

She had those dark and dreamy eyes
And she sang a song of love, sir,
She was one of those black-eyed bints,
She was one of the brigade.

Next there came the colonel's wife,
And she was dressed in red, sir,
And in her quite enormous quim,
She had a feather bed, sir.

CHORUS

Next there came the major's wife,
And she was dressed in pink, sir,
And in her quite enormous quim,
She had a kitchen sink, sir.

CHORUS

Next there came the captain's wife,
And she was dressed in blue, sir,
And in her quite enormous quim,
She had some four-by-two, sir.

CHORUS

Next there came the sergeant's wife,
And she was dressed in black, sir,
And in her quite enormous quim,
She had a chimney stack, sir.

CHORUS

Next there came the corporal's wife,
And she was dressed in brown, sir,
And in her quite enormous quim,
She had all Tidworth town, sir.

CHORUS

Trooper

The colonel's wife was dressing, a-dressing for a ball,
When she espied a trooper pissing up against the wall
With his bloody great kidney wiper,
His bloody great kidney beeze,
And forty yards of foreskin
Hanging down below his knees.

The lady wrote a letter, and in it she did say
She'd rather be fucked by the trooper than her old man
any day,
With his, *etc.*

He mounted on his charger, and on it he did ride,
With his bollocks in the saddle and his foreskin by his
side.
With his, *etc.*

He rode up to the mansion, he rode up to the hall,
'Cor Blimey,' said the butler, 'He's come to fuck us all.'
With his, *etc.*

He fucked the cook in the kitchen, the housemaids in the
hall,
He even fucked the tom-cat as it scrambled up the wall.
With his, *etc.*

Some say he's gone to heaven, some say he's gone to hell.
I hope he fucks the devil, and I know he'll fuck him well.
With his, *etc.*

Ivan Skavinsky Skavaar

This formerly unprintable, but amazingly widely known ballad of an epic fornicating contest properly belongs under Sods' Operas—see below.

The harems of Egypt were great to behold
And the women the fairest of fair,
But the fairest, a freak, was owned by a sheikh,
One Abdul the Bul Bul Emir.

Once a travelling brothel was brought to the town
By a Russian who came from afar.
And he issued a challenge to all who could shag,
Did Ivan Skavinsky Skavaar.

Thus Abdul did ride with a dame by his side,
His face was all flushed with desire,
And he wagered a thousand that he could outride
Count Ivan Skavinsky Skavaar.

The spectacle great was arranged for a date
When a visit was made by the Tsar,
And the streets were all lined with harlots entwined
With Ivan Skavinsky Skavaar.

They met on the track with tools hanging slack,
Till the starter's gun punctured the air.
Both quick on the rise, but all gaped at the size
Of Abdul the Bul Bul Emir.

The twats were all shorn and no Frenchies worn,
And Abdul's arse revved like a car.
But he hadn't a hope 'gainst the long even stroke
Of Ivan Skavinsky Skavaar.

When Ivan had won and was cleaning his gun,
He bent down to polish his pair,
When he felt a big poke on his old artichoke—
'Twas Abdul the Bul Bul Emir.

The harlots turned green. The men shouted 'Queen'.
They were ordered apart by the Tsar.
But fast they were stuck. 'Twas rotten hard luck
On Ivan Skavinsky Skavaar.

Mersa Matruh

There's a tavern in the town in Matruh,
There's a tavern in the town of Matruh.
There's a tavern in the town,
Where you lay your money down,
And you get a bit of brown,
In Matruh, in Matruh, in Matruh.

There's no paper in the bogs in Matruh.
There's no paper in the bogs in Matruh.
There's no paper in the bogs,
They just leave it till it clogs,
Then they saw it up in logs,
In Matruh, in Matruh, in Matruh.

There's a shortage of good bints in Matruh.
There's a shortage of good bints in Matruh.
There's a shortage of good bints,
So you pull it till you wince,
Then you tie it up in splints,
In Matruh, in Matruh, in Matruh.

The kitehawks, they fly high in Matruh.
The kitehawks, they fly high in Matruh.
The kitehawks they fly high,
Then they swoop down from the sky
And they shit right in your eye,
In Matruh, in Matruh, in Matruh.

There's a shortage of good whores in Matruh.
There's a shortage of good whores in Matruh.
There's a shortage of good whores,
But there's knot-holes in the floors
In Matruh, in Matruh, in Matruh.

All the ladies wear tin pants in Matruh.
All the ladies wear tin pants in Matruh.
All the ladies wear tin pants,
When they take them off to dance,
Every swaddy grabs his chance,
In Matruh, in Matruh, in Matruh.

8

The Concert Party

Despite the best efforts of ENSA * and of the finest singers, comedians and actors in the land who gave of their services, most men in the forces were starved of professional entertainment. Even those stationed in England couldn't often afford a ninepenny seat in the local fleapit: and in the desert, there weren't any fleapits.

Junior officers, feeling the need to arrange entertainments of some kind to mollify the 'other ranks', organised amateur concert parties in the camps and on the troopships. They meant well with their recitations, sketches and songs. But most of the humour that resulted was of the unintentional kind; and in any case, the constraints placed on the performers by the need for official approval for their material, and the presence of officers and ladies in the front rows, made the material anodyne. It wasn't easy to persuade 'other ranks' to appear on the makeshift stages at all, knowing as they did that they would be mercilessly ragged afterwards by their mates in the audience.

But for all that, the concert party was as integral a part of military life in the 1940s and 1950s as it was of village life in the Edwardian era, and at least something from it deserves to be preserved. Here, then, are three fairly typical items.

Won't it be Wonderful

English girls with eager lips,
WON'T IT BE WONDERFUL THEN.
Bass on draught with fish and chips,
WON'T IT BE WONDERFUL THEN.
The folks at home will revel in the 'bright-out',
And once again we'll all enjoy a perfect London night
out,

* Entertainments National Service Association.

Without the fear of wardens crying, 'Put that bloody
light out.'
WON'T IT BE WONDERFUL THEN.

Girls once more in silky white,
WON'T IT BE WONDERFUL THEN.
Every night a ladies' night,
WON'T IT BE WONDERFUL THEN.
When we draw near Blighty's shore with visions of a
cutie
We'll signal (with the Nelson touch) to England, home
and beauty,
'The MEF* expects each dame this night will do her
duty.'
WON'T IT BE WONDERFUL THEN.

No more cries of 'George—baksheesh!'
WON'T IT BE WONDERFUL THEN.
No more Sam with beer *mafeesh*,
WON'T IT BE WONDERFUL THEN.
We'll buy our suits in Savile Row—the best they can
create.
And cable Colonel Catherall, no matter what the rate
To stick his scale of clothing up his G1098.
WON'T IT BE WONDERFUL THEN.

No more thoughts of stripes and pips,
WON'T IT BE WONDERFUL THEN.
No more NAAFI eggs and chips,
WON'T IT BE WONDERFUL THEN.
We'll go out on a pub crawl, and when we've had our
spot.

* Middle East Forces.

We'll buy up all the eggs and bread that London's stores have got
And at the Gyppo Embassy we'll chuck the bloody lot.
WON'T IT BE WONDERFUL THEN.

Good old English grub to gorge,
WON'T IT BE WONDERFUL THEN.
No more cries of 'Clean boots, George?'
WON'T IT BE WONDERFUL THEN.
Production drives are over, and no one blames a shirker.
Colonels in the West End clubs devour the *Daily Worker*.
And in our honour Jermyn Street has been renamed the Berka.
WON'T IT BE WONDERFUL THEN.

No more queuing up for clothes,
WON'T IT BE WONDERFUL THEN.
No more changing well-worn hose,
WON'T IT BE WONDERFUL THEN.
We'll buy our socks at Austin Reed's, and all the world we'll show
We've not forgotten salvage schemes and anti-waste and so
We'll wrap the old socks up and send them out to Colonel Lowe.
WON'T IT BE WONDERFUL THEN.

Far from Cairo's sights and sounds,
WON'T IT BE WONDERFUL THEN.
No more places Out of Bounds,
WON'T IT BE WONDERFUL THEN.
Officers whose dignity most things are now beneath,
Cut off from their Gezira will be fed up to the teeth,
When they have to spend their weekends once again on 'Ampstead 'Eath.
WON'T IT BE WONDERFUL THEN.

No more workless, no distress,
WON'T IT BE WONDERFUL THEN.
So they tell us in the press,
WON'T IT BE WONDERFUL THEN.
The thing they call the Beveridge Plan will surely have to go.
When we get back to Blighty—we want them all to know
We wish no part of Beveridge—we want our Uncle Joe.
WON'T IT BE WONDERFUL THEN.

Cosy beds and snow-white sheets,
WON'T IT BE WONDERFUL THEN.
No more parking in the streets,
WON'T IT BE WONDERFUL THEN.
In London Transport buses as we crawl through Camden Town
We'll think of dear old Cairo and make the driver frown
Crying '*Mafeesh* all the traffic lights and mow the bastards down.'
WON'T IT BE WONDERFUL THEN.

No more orders from AG,*
WON'T IT BE WONDERFUL THEN.
No more bumph from C2E,
WON'T IT BE WONDERFUL THEN.
To remind us all of Cairo when this little show is through
We'll take a stroll at feeding time around the London Zoo,
For memories of the mealtime in the mess at GHQ.
WON'T IT BE WONDERFUL THEN.

---

* Adjutant-General.

Drinking toasts in British beer,
WON'T IT BE WONDERFUL THEN.
Meeting chaps we knew out here.
WON'T IT BE WONDERFUL THEN.
We might find Mr Burchall, the worthy CSM,
Outside the Empire, Leicester Square. Our joy we'll never stem
When we see his shining brasses bear the letters MGM.
WON'T IT BE WONDERFUL THEN.

No more queuing up for flicks,
WON'T IT BE WONDERFUL THEN.
No more bites from bugs and ticks,
WON'T IT BE WONDERFUL THEN.
In picture houses wooden chairs our pleasures will not blunt
While watching Betty Grable in a swim-suit in a punt,
Without the smell of garlic from the bints who sit in front.
WON'T IT BE WONDERFUL THEN.

No more girls in uniform,
WON'T IT BE WONDERFUL THEN.
Backless gowns and hair unshorn,
WON'T IT BE WONDERFUL THEN.
When they step out of khaki and parade around the City
And they can bare their lovely limbs, and other things as pretty
And strip without the thought of being stripped by Mrs Chitty,
WON'T IT BE WONDERFUL THEN.

Drill's the Thing

To the tune of 'The Red Flag'

While battles rage and cannons roar,
The foul Hun's spilling Russian gore.
The Free French die, Norwegians too.
Is that concern for me and you?
The foreigners don't understand
That drill's the thing that rules the land.
For wherever we are on land or sea
The time is always 'One, Two, Three'.

While Chinese dead lie stiff as boards,
The east's o'errun by Nippon's hordes.
The Philipinos lost the fight
Because they don't know left from right,
And although they're brave and fit and fleet,
They never used to stamp their feet.
For wherever we are on land or sea,
The time is always 'One, Two, Three'.

The Dutch who ruled on Java's isle
Had to leave for quite a while
The cause of this there is no doubt
Was their improper kit layout.
The OCTU lads, you must agree,
Are quite the smartest squad you'll see.
For wherever we are on land or sea
The time is always 'One, Two, Three'.

Australian troops, though most astute,
Are useless at the front salute,
And though New Zealand men can fight,
They never give a good eyes-right.
But drill's the thing, there is no doubt
To beat the Jap and Nazi lout.
For wherever we are on land or sea
The time is always 'One, Two, Three'.

Written in 1942 on a troopship going to India

If

If you can fold a greatcoat
In the Pakapura style,
If you can shine a mirror
That'll make sergeant-major smile,
If you can fold a blanket
And sweep a floor as well,
If you can lay your kit out
And lay your kit out well,
If you can polish buttons,
And polish away like hell,
If you can make a bed
And get rid of a cupboard smell,

If you can scrub a cabin floor
And dust the walls as well,
If you can fold a lifebelt
And fold a lifebelt well,
Then my lad it seems to me
You need not know your drill,
And if you cannot shoot or fight
Your worries should be nil.

In the east particularly, the shortage of professional entertainers for the troops led the authorities to ask for volunteers from among those on active service to form touring companies. One such company was ACES (Amenities, Comforts and Entertainments for the services).

An Indian journalist wrote in 1943: 'For nearly a year now, ACES have been touring all over India and Ceylon, in heat, rain and dust, carrying with them portable stages.

'Each show contains eight British sergeants who also, besides playing in the shows and the band, control costumes, curtains, lighting and the erection of the stages.

'Shows go on in spite of severe handicaps e.g. rain on hangar roofs drowning the singers, lorry accidents: very often no electricity means petromax or hurricane lamps. Under grease paint, a torrid night sky, the heat is sometimes overpowering—but the show goes on.

'The greatest strain is on the girls who dance and sing to the troops under varying and rarely pleasant conditions. Under canvas, in temporary shelters, sharing the Tommies' bully beef, iron rations, and sometimes no chance of a bath for days on end, these pioneers carry on the work of breaking the monotony of camp life to the soldier "out in the blue".

'They arrive in trucks or bullock carts and very often they are the first girls the boys have seen for years. When Private —— takes his four-anna seat that evening and stares up at the fluttering blue curtains in the evening breeze, he is immediately taken "back home" for a couple of hours.

Through the haze of the hurricane lamps, he hears jokes about his home town, hears songs his folks sing . . .

'The gruelling work, the constant travelling and hardship is all offset by the great receptions the troops give these ACES shows . . . Sometimes when rations are short they perform on nothing more than a cup of tea before entertaining again at night to travel through the small hours to reach another out of the way station to open again . . .

'Many are the backstage heartaches which have to be masked when the curtain goes up. One comedian, a sergeant from the Midlands, while performing in Northern India, received a cable to say he had lost his mother in an air raid back home. But he bounded on to the stage and cracked his usual opening jokes about air-raid shelters.'

9

Sods' Operas

The Oozlum bird that could whistle the national anthem through its arsehole, the angel who was chocker with 'arpin' and the dirty-minded prophet who threw lion's dung at a king may seem, on first acquaintance, to have little to do with life in the armed forces. They were, in fact, some of the leading characters from the repertoire of that revered military institution, the Sods' Opera.

Sods' Operas were staged, somewhat secretly, to supplement the rather stultified entertainment that was offered officially. Away from the hearing of officers, they flourished in the wet canteen and on the mess decks of ships.

There was the male striptease (innocent of any homosexual content). There was the mock lantern-slide show, *The Menagerie*, whose origins go back to the First World War but which was revived and remained popular throughout the second.

And there were the monologues—including *'Arpin'*, *'Ardship* and *Daniel and the King.*

I believe this to be the first time that any of these classics of the genre have been published.

YOU'RE NOT 'ARF AS FED UP OF 'ARPIN AS I AM, MATE!

This Old Hat of Mine

The venerated ritual of the barrack-room striptease has received scant attention from military commentators.

A fully-dressed soldier stood on a table on which there was also a pint of beer.

Coyly, he removed his hat, waved it over his head and plunged it into the beer, singing:

Now this old hat of mine,
It's been out on the line.
We'll dip it in the wine—
It's had its bleeding time.

And so he went on, removing his clothes one by one and plunging them into the beer as he sang the song, substituting the appropriate word for each article of clothing.

When he was completely naked, as a finale he drank down what was left of the beer, by then in a disgusting state.

The Menagerie

Good evening, ladies and gentlemen. You can see before you the fabulous Phoenix. This North African bird, when feeling the approach of his end, flies round a tall palm tree in circles of decreasing radius and increasing velocity, finally flying up its own arsehole with a loud report and a cloud of smoke.

Ernie, turn the crank.

This is the Oozlum bird, normally quite dumb. But when excited it sticks its long bill into the mud of the seashore and whistles *God Save the King* out of its arse—hence the Trade Winds.

Ernie, turn the crank.

Here we have the Hippopotamus, whose hide is so tough that no bullet can pierce, no spear penetrate. How, then, is it overcome? Ah ha! The wily natives are up to the dodge: they apply ginger to its touch-hole. Up goes the tail—and in go the arrows. Not one, mind you, but in thousands: and the whole show is over.

Ernie, turn the crank.

The Rhinoceros, ladies and gentlemen, is the richest animal in the world. Rhino = money. Sore arse = piles. Piles of money.

Ernie, turn the crank.

This large ape, the Orang Utang, inhabits the impenetrable forests of Borneo, but when overcome by his lust, descends to the plains in search of village maidens. He finds, feels, fondles and finally fucks them, exclaiming the while, in his own language, 'yahoo, yahoo',—which being interpreted, means 'By God, that's good'.

Ernie, turn the crank.

I would draw your attention to the Tight-skinned Parrot. His skin is so tight that when he closes his eyes, he skins his prick, a drawback he bears with an equanimity amounting to delight. His eyes are now closed, hence the odd smell. Madam, please stop your small boy throwing sand at him to make him blink.

Ernie, turn the crank.

Finally, the Camel, who comes from the mighty Sahara Desert, where normal food is scarce. He eats sand, has a triangular arse and shits bricks. Hence the pyramids.

Thank you, Ernie.

'Arpin'

During the battle of the Atlantic, there were two stokers serving in a destroyer. One of them was a very bad man but the other, whose name was Hawkins, was a very good man.

When the destroyer was torpedoed and sunk with all hands, the bad stoker was not at all surprised to find himself in hell. He was greatly surprised, a few days later, while he was on watch stoking the infernal boilers, to find his former shipmate Hawkins coming to join him with a shovel over his shoulder.

''Allo mate,' he said. 'What're you doin' 'ere? I thought you was sure to go to 'Eaven.'

'So I did,' said Hawkins. 'But it didn't seem to work out right.'

''Ow was that, then?' asked his mate.

'Well, it was like this,' said Hawkins. 'When the tin fish gets us, I finds myself outside the gates of 'Eaven, where they seems to be expecting me. So I goes in, carries out me joinin' routine, draws me 'arp, me wings and me 'alo, what I signs for, slings me 'ammock on a bit of cloud and gets turned in.

'Next morning, after Divisions, the Seraph-Major starts telling off parties from the right-'and end of the line. "'Ere to 'ere, Pearly Gates polishin' party. 'Ere to 'ere, Fiery Chariots wheel-greasin'. 'Ere to 'ere, Lord God's messengers. Remainder, 'arpin'."

'So I 'arps from then to stand-easy, from stand-easy to dinner-time and from after dinner till we secure for the day. And by then I'm getting pretty chocker with 'arpin'.

'So next day I gets fell in on the right, but the Leadin' Angel takes 'is parties from the left-'and end—"'Ere to 'ere, Pearly Gates polishin' party. 'Ere to 'ere, Fiery Chariots wheel-greasin'. 'Ere to 'ere, Lord God's messengers. Remainder, 'arpin'."

'So once again I 'arps until stand-easy, then till dinner, then till we secure and by then I'm very chocker with 'arpin'.

'So next day, I gets fell in in the middle. And the Leadin' Angel takes two of his parties from the right, and two from the left, and us in the middle, it's "Remainder, 'arpin'."

'Well, by then I'd 'ad enough. So I throws down me 'arp on a cloud and says, "I'm chocker with 'arpin'."

'The Seraph-Major comes over and says, "'Awkins, you was ordered to 'arp."

' "Yes, Chief," I says, "but I'm chocker with 'arpin'."

' "Very well," 'e says. "Archangel's report."

'So the next morning, the Master at 'Arps marches me in before the duty Archangel an' says: "Actin' Angel 'Awkins, sir, did act to the prejudice of good order and 'Eavenly discipline in that 'e did refuse to 'arp."

' "Anything to say?" says the Archangel.

' "I'm sorry, sir," I says, "but I'm chocker with 'arpin'."

' "Very well," 'e says. "Creator's report."

'So next morning, I'm up before the Creator 'imself. The Master at 'Arps marches me in.

' "Actin' Angel 'Awkins, off 'alo. Actin' Angel 'Awkins, sir, did act to the prejudice of good order and 'Eavenly discipline in that 'e did refuse to 'arp."

' "Well?" says the Creator.

' "Well, sir," I says, most respectful. "I'm sorry sir, but I'm chocker with 'arpin'."

' "Now look 'ere 'Awkins," 'e says, "everybody what comes to 'Eaven 'as to do 'is 'arpin'. Now why can't you do it?"

' "I'm very sorry, sir," I says, "but I'm chocker with 'arpin'."

' "Very well, 'Awkins," says the Creator. "If that's the way it is, there's nothing else I can do. Three days 'Ell."

'So 'ere I am.'

'Ardship

This young sailor went into a pub in Portsmouth.

'Hello, sailor,' said the barmaid. 'What ship are you from then?'

''Ardship,' he replied.

''Ardship?' cut in an old sailor sitting alone in the corner. ''Ardship? You don't know what 'ardship is.

'When I signed on, I was sent to this old ship. It was the filthiest fucking ship in the Navy. And the first thing they tell us to do is to clean the fucking thing. For three fucking weeks we had to scrub and scrape and paint it before it could even put to sea.

''Ardship? You don't know what 'ardship is.

'Then we sailed out into the Atlantic and got caught in the worst storm ever. For three fucking weeks we were in that storm.

''Ardship? You don't know what 'ardship is.

'And then the ship went down. There weren't enough life-rafts. So I grabbed hold of a rope fixed to the side of one and hung on. For three fucking weeks I hung on to that rope.

''Ardship? You don't know what 'ardship is.

'Then the life-raft broke to pieces in the storm and we had to swim. For three fucking weeks I had to swim.

''Ardship? You don't know what 'ardship is.

'Then I got to this desert island. I was too weak to walk, so I crawled. For three fucking weeks I crawled.

''Ardship? You don't know what 'ardship is.

'I got to this cottage, and I crawled up to the door and banged on it. Nobody answered. For three fucking weeks, I banged on that door.

''Ardship? You don't know what 'ardship is.

'Then the door opened. An old lady was standing there. "Food," I cried. "Give me food." But she was deaf and couldn't hear me. For three fucking weeks I shouted at her before she understood me.

"Ardship? You don't know what 'ardship is.

'She went out the back, and came back with a handful of flour, dry flour, and gave it to me. I asked her for some water to mix with it so I could eat it. For three fucking weeks I shouted "Water" at her before she understood me.

"Ardship? You don't know what 'ardship is.

'She took me to her well. It hadn't been used for years. The handle was so stiff you could hardly move it. I heaved and I pushed to pull the bucket up. For three fucking weeks I heaved and I pushed.

"Ardship? You don't know what 'ardship is.

'The bucket came up and it was empty. Not having any water in me myself, I shouted to the old lady to pee on the flour to wet it for me. I shouted and shouted. For three fucking weeks I shouted at her.

"Ardship? You don't know what 'ardship is.

'She pulled up her skirt. I held the flour between her legs. And she grunted and strained. For three fucking weeks she grunted and strained.

"Ardship? You don't know what 'ardship is.

'After three weeks, she farted and all the flour blew away.

"Ardship? You don't know what 'ardship is.'

Daniel and the King

Now it came to pass that the King came unto the prophet Daniel where he abode in the lion's den and spake unto him, saying, How is it with thee, O Daniel? And Daniel answered and said unto the King, Lo, O King, it locks.
What locks? asked the King, suspecting naught.
Bollocks, roared Daniel: and the drinks were on the King.

And on the second day, the King came again unto Daniel and spake again unto him, saying, How is it with thee, O Daniel? And Daniel answered and said unto the King, Lo, O King, it tickles.
What tickles? asked the King, for he feared no ill.
Testicles, roared Daniel: and once again the drinks were on the King.

Now the King became exceeding vexed and betook to himself a plan whereby he might fool the prophet: and on the third day, he came again unto Daniel and spake again unto him, saying, O Daniel, how is it with thee in yonder hole? But Daniel, being wiser than the King, stole the punchline the King had deviseth so he fell not into the trap the King had laith by saying unto him, What hole, O King? Straightway he roared Arsehole: and on the third day again, the drinks were on the King.

Now Daniel, becoming weary of these visitations, on the fourth day took unto himself a dollop of lion's dung of the bigness of a cubit and a span and did hurl it at the King, and smote him betwixt the eyes.
Shit, cried the King, and the whole court bent their knees and *strained*, for that they dared do no other.

Here endeth the lesson.

They're pulling down the Pub

They're pulling down the old pub!
CHORUS: *Boo!*
And building a new one three times as big!
CHORUS: *Hurray!*
There won't be no barmaids.
CHORUS: *Boo!*
There'll be twenty-five brown-hats serving behind the counter instead.
CHORUS: *Hurray!*
There's not going to be any beer.
CHORUS: *Boo!*
But whisky's going to be threepence a pint.
CHORUS: *Hurray!*
They're pouring it all down the sink.
CHORUS: *Boo!*
We're going down to the river,
We're going down to the river,
We're going down to the river,
To drink from the canteen sink.

Recitation in the manner of Nancy, Lady Astor, addressing the House of Commons

We want what men can give us, and we will force them to give it to us if need be. It may not be much but we want it. (*Cheers*)

We will have it with or without friction, and if we cannot have it through our organisations we will have it through our combinations—with or without them if necessary. (*Loud cheers*) We refuse to be poked up in the gallery (cries of *Shame*). And we insist upon being put on the floor of the House. (*Interruptions*)

Are we going to take it lying down? NO!!! We will take it with our backs to the wall.

A drunken loafer may shout: 'Down with petticoats.' We say: 'Up with petticoats, down with trousers.' Only then will things become visible in their true light. After all, there is little difference between a man and a woman. (*Voices*: 'Three cheers for the little difference.')

Furthermore, we may say that so long as we remain split up as we are, the men will try to get on top of us. (*Applause*)

10

Bolshies

Army officers, or regular soldiers of any rank for that matter, are not known for any love of 'progressive' left-wing ideologies. And it was to their considerable consternation that they found, on Hitler invading Russia and the USSR and Britain thus becoming involuntary allies, that the conscripts they were given to fight with were riddled with red revolutionaries from the industrial heartlands of Britain.

The army was not in the habit of arguing the toss with other ranks, and these barrack-room bolsheviks became an irremovable thorn in its flesh. They preached dissidence in the billets and planted subversive tracts in the camp libraries. Later, during the Malayan campaign against the pro-Chinese guerrillas, some decided for themselves that they had no quarrel with communism and found surreptitious means of undermining the British drive against it.

It was the persistence of this attitude among some conscripts that weighed heavily on the high command in its pleas with the Government to abolish call-up in favour of a smaller professionally loyal army.

During World War II itself there was sufficient dissidence in some ranks to cause a serious problem of morale. Workers' Internationalism manifested itself even in the Western Desert: and the notion that they had been put there not to fight against evil on behalf of a lofty ideal but because it suited the merchants of death and capitalism in general was assiduously put about by the 8th Army's self-appointed shop-stewards to some effect.

At one stage, Durham miners threatened to strike. The British press lambasted them for putting their own selfish, material interests above the lives of the men at the front—without coal, there could be no steel, without steel, no weapons and ammunition, and without those, the lads in the desert would be defenceless and massacred by the Germans. An unofficial opinion poll conducted in one front-line unit by a journalist who was not a socialist found an overwhelming majority of the lads to be in support of the miners for striking, a blow against the bosses on whose behalf, they claimed to believe, they were being made to fight.

It was held by this element that the enemies were not the German soldiers on the other side of the sand dunes but the systems which had placed them, weapons in hand, face to face with one another—that the views of Churchill and Hitler and their respective establishments might differ in detail, but fundamentally their interest was in conducting an imperialistic war against the interests of the proletariat.

All this reads rather quaintly now, but it was real enough then to worry those in command. It is a topic which was not publicly reported or discussed at the time, for obvious reasons, and perhaps as a result has been barely remarked upon since.

So in retrospect it is hard to gauge how serious the bolshiness among the conscripts was.

However, there is no question but that British soldiers captured by the Germans who escaped back to their own lines returned, in many cases, with stories of the friendly, indeed comradely treatment that they had received from those of equivalent rank on the German side, and that such stories made a deep and demoralising impression. Similarly, many British troops, fed as they had been with propaganda about the fundamental bestiality of the German character, were favourably struck by conversations they had with Afrika Korps troopers they captured.

It was rumoured, indeed, that one Highland regiment was so struck that they briefly refused to take part in the fighting against fellow members of the working class.

Whether or not this was true—it's not the kind of incident that finds its way into regimental histories—there is an impressive piece of circumstantial evidence that the authorities were alarmed by the existence of such attitudes, which I found in a yellowing copy of *The Crusader*, the official newspaper of the Desert Army.

It was a forcefully projected article, clearly officially inspired, entitled *Don't Be Fooled By Jerry.*

'There are several kinds of bonehead who are dangerous to us in this war,' it began mildly enough. 'One of these is the chap who goes around saying: "Jerry is a pretty good chap, really . . ."

'No sensible person suggests that the average German is a monster,' it continued (though that was exactly what some official propaganda did say). 'Germans are average, quiet, decent folk if left to themselves. But they are never left to themselves. It is never the quiet, decent German who gets to the top in Germany—it's the ruthless bullies who get there . . .

'It has been the same old story for generations. And through it all the man upon whom these bullies have relied to make their savage dreams come true is the German soldier, the common-or-garden Jerry.

'Not a bad chap, taken by himself. Well, the writer met a quiet, ordinary-looking chap in Chicago. His hobbies were billiards and Italian opera. He looked like a fairly prosperous businessman.

'He was a "cannon" for Al Capone.

'He had no personal feeling against the people he "bumped off"—he just obeyed orders from "The Boss" . . .

'The German has long prided himself on being a good soldier—which to him means above all doing what he is told.

'If he is ordered to behave politely to the inhabitants of a conquered country, he will step off the pavements to make way for your wife and help your kiddies on to the bus.

'But if he is told to treat the inhabitants with "ruthless severity", as the official Nazi phrase goes, he will hang your wife in the town square and machine-gun your kiddies in batches . . .

'He will be used to enslave our own people, unless enough Jerries, "decent" or otherwise, are put under the earth or in the prisoners' cage.'

The fact that the Red Army was also fighting the Germans did something to alleviate the situation in North Africa. But the feeling was still fairly widespread that in those circumstances, the real reason for polishing off the Germans was so that the 8th Army could then go home, overthrow Churchill and his gang, and proclaim the workers' paradise.

Meanwhile, in song and verse, these desert revolutionaries proclaimed their disdain for their own leader, their worship of 'Uncle Joe' Stalin and their deprecation of the British fighting man compared with those of the Red Army.

Uncle Joe

To the tune of 'The Lincolnshire Poacher'

Oh Hitler's a non-smoker, and Churchill smokes cigars,
And they're both as keen as mustard on imperialistic
wars.
But your Uncle Joe's a worker and a very decent chap
Because he smokes a pipe and wears
A taxi-driver's cap.

When Rommel got to Alamein and shook the British
line,
The whole of Cairo beat it to the land of Palestine.
But Moscow's never raised a yell, and never had a flap,
Because Joe smokes a pipe and wears
A taxi-driver's cap.

That Hitler's armies can't be beat is just a lot of cock,
For Marshal Timoshenko's boys are pissing through Von
Bock.
The Führer makes the bloomers, and his marshals take
the rap.
Meanwhile Joe smokes a pipe and wears
A taxi-driver's cap.

The fascist drive on Stalingrad is going mighty slow,
They've hit a room in number nine of Slobbenskaya
Row.
When fascist armies start to run, old Goebbels fills the
gap.
Meanwhile Joe smokes a pipe and wears
A taxi-driver's cap.

At home those buggers publicise the deeds of 'Our Ally'.
Their dearest wish was once to biff the Bolshies in the eye.
Your Uncle Joe is wise to this. He isn't such a sap—
Although he smokes a pipe and wears
A taxi-driver's cap.

Thank God for the Red Army

Tommy thinks he holds Tobruk.
Along the road comes Rommel.
Inside two shakes Tobruk is took
And Tommy's on the bummel.

He's on the bummel to the Rhine
Where sylphs will drive him barmy.
I think old Timoshenko's fine.
Thank God for the Red Army!

Liberty!

One day, Private Sarky, brave and bold,
Asked Sarge if it's true what he'd been told,
That Freedom is what we're fighting for.

'Of course, of course,' said Sarge there and then,
'I'll say you are. Now listen you men
You've got to be British to the core.

'So get on with your work, no slacking now.
If I catch yer scrounging you're for it, and how!
You'd bloody well better win, otherwise you'll be for it.'

Gratitude

These verses are about a purely Australian row, and are bitter indeed.

A certain statement caught my eye
In a recent *Guinea Gold.*
And when I read the story
I confess it left me cold.

It was the lamentation
Of New Guinea goldmine groups
That some of their most precious ore
Had gone home with the troops.

They fled back home to Aussie
When the Japs attacked this isle:
They wouldn't fight for what they owned—
It wasn't worth their while.

They sat back in their offices,
If you get what I mean.
They wouldn't wear the old slouch hat
Or a suit of jungle green.

They visited the Stock Exchange
And shook with agitation
When they saw their shares come tumbling down
In market fluctuation.

And then their frowns were turned to smiles
When news at last came back
That the Japs were fast retreating
Along the Salamanaua track.

They cared not for the boys who died
Upon their goldfield ground
But many heroes sleep at Wau
Beneath a hallowed mound.

The lads returned to Aussie
To the cities' fervent cheers
And showed their friends some nuggets
That they'd brought as souvenirs.

The whisper soon got to the heads
Of all these goldmine groups,
And soon they wailed: 'We're being robbed
By these returning troops.'

They didn't give us credit
For the work the boys had done
In taking their most valued stock
Back from the Rising Sun.

Then Federal members took their case
And backed it man to man—
The same men who exported
Our scrap iron to Japan.

So they read an Act in Parliament
Without one single flaw
Which said that taking gold back home
Was not within the law.

And so the diggers read it,
And shrugged, and gave a grin.
You could slaughter all the Japs you liked
But to take gold was a sin.

Some day we'll see those businessmen
And we'll ram it in their head
That many men did not get gold,
But died, with lead, instead.

11

Korea: When the Ice is on the Rice

No large-scale action fought by British conscripts in World War II was more bitter than that in which their 'peace-time' successors, the national servicemen, fought in Korea between 1950 and 1953, alongside Australians, Canadians, New Zealanders, a huge force of Americans and other nationalities. And World War II produced few songs as forlorn as those that came out of this miserable conflict.

The Korean War was not conducive to that jovial camaraderie, that larking about that a later generation of film and television producers has attributed to World War II, to the delight of vast audiences still. Perhaps this is why this last major conflict in which British conscripts were engaged is, if not actually forgotten, so rarely portrayed and discussed these days, and why so little is known of it.

On 25 June 1950 North Korean troops poured without warning over the 38th Parallel. Seoul, the southern capital, fell to them three days later.

The non-communist world doubted for hardly a moment that the Russians were behind the attack and that if it was allowed to succeed, it would prove to be but the first move in a new campaign of Soviet expansionism.

Within hours of the first shots being fired, the United Nations Security Council met in New York and, after cursory debate, resolved a motion calling upon all members to condemn the 'action of aggression' and to send troops to 'assist in the securing of peace'.

To the tune of 'Galway Bay'

When the ice is on the rice upon the Yalu,
And the Chinaman is creeping up on you,
I'll send you a pretty little postcard
While I'm sitting on my arse in Wi Jong Bhu.

The Americans were the sponsors, and Britain, Australia, Canada and New Zealand were among the first to respond. An international force under General MacArthur arrived in July.

After some early reverses, MacArthur managed to cut off a sizeable number of the northern invaders by means of an amphibious assault. By 1 October he had reached the 38th Parallel, and the General jubilantly announced to war correspondents that 'the boys will be home by Christmas'.

At the time, it seemed a reasonable enough prediction. Pyongyang, the northern capital, fell to the UN troops on 20 October, and they reached the banks of the Yalu River, on the border with the Chinese province of Manchuria, six days later.

But then China, with one and a half million of its own troops massed on the other side of the river, intervened, fearing invasion otherwise. MacArthur, no man for the observance of political and diplomatic niceties, publicly and loudly declared in defiance of UN and American policy that the only solution was to cross the border and smash the Red Chinese on their own territory. He was promptly fired by a President who had already put up with a lot from an irascible if brilliant commander.

MacArthur's plan was beyond consideration—the chances that it would spark off World War III were too great. But the alternative, even if it was the only one, was terrible. For a further two years and nine months, the war raged on until, in July 1953, a truce was signed, leaving the country divided almost exactly as it had been before, the difference being that it was now devastated.

Even those who resented the fact that they were obliged to devote some of the best years of their lives to fighting fascism in World War II, even those who are disillusioned by the shape the postwar world assumed, cannot question at the end of the day that good came out of it and that a very real menace to humanity was decisively destroyed. But those who fought in Korea has no such gratification. Even the most fervent anti-communists could claim no more than that communism had been pushed back to its boundaries of three years earlier: and perhaps most of those Britons and others who pushed them back were under no illusion that in doing so, they had struck a blow for freedom and democracy against totalitarianism. 'Fighting for that bastard, Syngman Rhee,'* is how one song put it, 'Guarding over the millionaires for lousy shillings a day,' another expressed it.

In the process Britain alone suffered 4,451 casualties, Canada 257, New Zealand 111 and the United States 142,227. As a proportion of the population, American casualties were 113 times greater than ours and over two thousand times greater than New Zealand's. But for the British fighting there, only five years after the end of the war to end all wars, the losses seemed all the worse because the cause itself, fought in defence of a regime of dubious morality in a distant land, was that much less compelling.

Hence the lack of rowdy reunions of nostalgic Korean War veterans in the Albert Hall.

* The South Korean Dictator.

That Bastard Syngman Rhee

When I was in New Zealand,
Having lots of fun,
A war broke out in Korea,
They handed me a gun,
Just to fight for that bastard, Syngman Rhee.

We landed at Pusan,
It wasn't very nice,
We didn't come to Korea
To eat your mouldy rice,
But to fight for that bastard, Syngman Rhee.

Oh my feet are weary
From travelling dusty roads.
Oh my back is aching
From carrying heavy loads,
'Cause I'm fighting for that bastard, Syngman Rhee.

The Blood on the Hills of Korea

There is blood on the hills of Korea,
'Tis the blood of the brave and the true,
Where the 29th Brigade battled together
'Neath the banner of red, white and blue.

As they marched over the fields of Korea,
To the hills where the enemy lay.
They remembered the Brigadier's orders:
'Those hills must be taken today.'

Forward they marched into battle
With faces unsmiling and stern.
They knew as they marched up the hillsides
There were some who would never return.

Some thought of their wives and mothers,
Some thought of their sweethearts so fair,
And some, as they plodded and stumbled,
Were softly whispering a prayer.

There is blood on the hills of Korea.
It's their gift to the freedom they love.
May their names live in glory for ever
And their souls rest in heaven above.

Moving On

If there's any two things that I can't stand,
It's a North Korean and a Chinaman.
We're moving on, we're moving on.

See the Chinkies coming up 355,
The Yanks pulling out in overdrive,
They're moving on, they're moving on.

See the Kiwi guns pointing in the air,
But the Kiwi gunners, they're not there.
They're moving on, they're moving on.

See the Chinese soldiers coming over the ridge,
Heading like hell for the Pintail Bridge,
They're moving on, they're moving on.

Ashes to ashes, and dust to dust,
If the Chinks don't get you the Asahi* must.
We're moving on, we're moving on.

* A brand of Japanese beer.

Our Mess on the Hill

We are building a mess on the hill,
We are building a mess on the hill.
We'll never say die
While we've got CGI
And the Sappers are footing the bill.

If you come to Rear Div. today
No doubt you'll be invited to stay,
You'll be knocked for a loop
By our self-heating soup,
And your jeeps will be stolen away
By the Kiwis from over the hill.

We are still building there on the hill,
Sustained by a Paludrine pill.
Though we work day and night,
Still the damned things not right,
And we wonder if ever it will.

Each Sunday we climb to Kamaksan
It's part of the S & T plan.
For we answer the call
Just to play volley-ball
And see the Kiwis fall
For the sake of our mess on the hill.

The Military Police Psalm (Korea)

The REDCAP is my shepherd. I shall not worry. He maketh me to lie down at 23.30 hours nightly. He leadeth me past the SAKE houses. I do not enter for he is right behind me. He prepareth me a 252 in the presence of my muckers. Yea, though I walk through the alleys in the shadow of the shacks, I need not fear him, for he shall not catch me. His boots and his blanco announceth him. And so I shall pass the rest of the night in glory, for mine is a cherry girl.

The Banks of the Imjin

To the tune of 'The Red River Valley'

'Tis down by the shores of the Imjin,
Where most of the fighting was done,
'Twas there that a Commonwealth soldier
Was shot by a communist gun.

As he raised himself on one elbow,
And the blood from his wounds it dripped red,
As he gazed at his comrades around him,
These were the last words he said.

'Bury me down by the Imjin
Under the Korean sun.
Bury me down by the Imjin,
For my duty to Country I've done.'

So they buried him down by the Imjin,
And a small wooden cross marks his grave,
And these were the words writ upon it:
'His young life for freedom he gave.'

12

Odds and Sods

Most of the contributions that came in to me formed themselves into neat ranks, under subject headings they themselves suggested.

A few did not, but nonetheless demanded inclusion.

The Ten Commandments

Who, or which group of servicemen, originally drafted the Soldier's Ten Commandments, nobody knows. But they were familiar to thousands: and although I don't find them brilliantly funny myself, others at the time clearly did.

In one form or another I received nine copies of them.

1 Thou shalt not take the name of thy sergeant-major in vain, or thou shalt have thy name enrolled on a 252 and be called upon to repent thy sin within the presence of the sergeants' mess amidst many dirty vessels.

2 Thou shalt not scrounge or try to swing the lead, lest thy resting place be the trough in which the horses quench their thirst.

3 Honour thy pay book and the quarter bloke, that thy credit be even as the sands of the desert.

4 Thou shalt not take unto thyself thy comrade's kit nor borrow thereof during his absence, or thou shalt have thy sins thrust upon thee by the quickness of the hand that blacketh the eye.

5 Thou shalt not fill thyself to overflowing with beer, lest, by royal warrant, thou shalt lose much peace, and the provost sergeant shall number thee amongst his flock. For is it not written: 'He that drinketh shall pull the roller'?

6 Thou shalt not fritter away thy worldly goods by playing banker, nap or pontoon, lest the provost sergeant be heard to say: 'Render unto me your names, and let the money remain where it lieth.'

7 Six days thou shalt labour and do all that thou hast to do: and on the seventh, shalt thou do twice as much.

8 And if it should come to pass that by thy zeal and sweat of thy brow, thy name be mentioned in regimental orders to be raised to the dizzy heights of acting unpaid lance-corporal, thou shalt present thyself at the dwelling place of the big noises, known as the Junior NCOs' Club, and crave thou that they accept liquid refreshment at thine own expense.

9 Thou shalt not kill the cook if he grieveth thee, nor devour the hand that feedeth thee to supplement thy meat ration, but thou shalt make the complaint through proper channels where man expecteth little and receiveth less.

10 And when it shall come to pass that thou art time expired, thou shalt clothe thyself in strange garments and pass into the street called 'Civvy'. There thou shalt study the dole and the drawing thereof, and lo, for many moons thou shalt rest from thy labours.

Corporal, Acting, Unpaid, Lance

Descend, O Muse, from Pelion's rocky height
Into the dark abysm of arctic night
Give ear to one who supplicates thine aid
To wit, myself, NATHANIEL BIGGLESWADE.
With stentorous echo let the welkin ring,
While I of honours and preferments sing.

I who erewhile with patient hands did clean
And disinfect the officers' latrine,
Who with a leaden heart and scant reprieve
Absterged and swept from morn to dewy eve,
I craved promotion, and promotion came
With rich addition to my humble name.

For now by strange reverse of Fortune's wheel
I wait upon the sergeants at each meal
Behind the bar, dispensing wet and dry
I stand, the cynosure of every eye.
Thanks, gracious goddess, multifarious chance,
For now I'm corporal, acting, unpaid, lance.

THAT MAN HAS A
FILTHY EYE, SERGEANT!

Generals ride in Cars

Under the fucking truck, chum,
Flat on me fucking back,
Right in the fucking muck, chum,
Stuck on the fucking track.
Generals ride in cars, chum,
Or go marching smartly by.
But I'm flat on my back on the fucking track,
With oil in me fucking eye.

Forces Food

There was the tasteless conscripts' story of the squaddy—the only one, ever—who found army food delicious.

Every mealtime he sniffed appreciatively at the odours of stale cabbage and congealed gristle stew that wafted towards him as he came into the canteen, held his plate out with smiles of anticipation, grunted with delight as he ate, and thanked the cooks heartily as he left.

The cooks responded to this unique challenge by giving him more and more disgusting platefuls, to no avail. Finally, in desperation, they gathered up some horse manure, dipped it in batter, fried it and gave it to him.

They gathered round to see his response.

Muttering with delight, he cut it with his knife, put a forkful into his mouth and munched enthusiastically.

After a moment he paused, inspected and then dissected the contents of his plate.

'It's horse shit!' he exclaimed. But then, looking up into the cooks' eyes, added, 'But beautifully cooked.'

Food was a matter of interminable dissension between the officers responsible for supervising its provision and the other ranks. The other ranks held that the thing to do was to swallow it down as best one could without complaining to higher authority, because you'd only get into trouble if you did. The officers concerned said that their charges had been so ill-trained at home in what a proper diet consisted of that they didn't know one when they saw one, and groused as a matter of principle, no matter what they were given: and that the more luxurious the food, the more they would carp at it.

It was true that when aubergines (which had yet to enjoy their vogue as the exotic vegetable of those who live in Islington, Battersea and Didsbury (Manchester) and collect their recipes from the colour supplements of the posh papers) were issued to the British in Egypt as their vegetable rations, there was quite a lot of trouble until the powers that be put out the news that they could be chipped and fried like potatoes.

But it is also true that Lord Marples, politician and gastronome, has told me that, when a sergeant-major, he himself considered the normal standards of army food to be disgusting, and therefore put himself on a cookery course run by a Mr Salmon of Lyons, returned to his unit and reorganised the kitchen into producing appetising food, with no change in the raw materials.

For all that, raw materials were in short supply, and the army's cooking experts tried to put over some fairly horrendous ideas that made civilian moaning about Woolton Pie and the like seem trivial.

The item of culinary psychological warfare that follows, was aimed at British troops in Iceland.

Appetising Recipe

Brown Rat

Stuff a young brown rat with a simple stuffing made of breadcrumbs, a sprinkling of sweet herbs, a little salt and pepper to taste and the heart and liver of the rat. Roast for a few minutes in a hot oven.

The result produces a very toothsome article of diet and a dish not unlike snipe in flavour.

Bumph

With Reference to
Your CRO 2E
Oblique stroke F
Oblique stroke G
Oblique stroke five
Oblique stroke four
Oblique stroke, figures
Five or more,
Here are the facts
For which you yearn:
Another fucking nil return.

Sergeant-Majors

To the tune of 'John Brown's Body'

Our Sergeant-Major's got a crown upon his arm.
Our Sergeant-Major's got a crown upon his arm.
Our Sergeant-Major's got a crown upon his arm.
And he thinks he's got it on his fucking head.

Our Flight-Sergeant wants a rope around his neck.
Our Flight-Sergeant wants a rope around his neck.
Our Flight-Sergeant wants a rope around his neck.
And we'll all give a bloody great pull.

I do not like the sergeant's face,
I do not like his chatter.
And what I think about his brain
Is censorable matter.
He sits in a tent
At the end of a street
And clutters his desk
With his oversized feet.
I do not like the sergeant's nose.
It would look better broken.
I do not like his tone of voice
When drill commands are spoken.
I do not like the sergeant's view
On army life and such
But what I think about the sarge
Doesn't seem to matter much.

The Sergeant

'Now don't get up,' the sergeant said.
'Please don't get up for me.
I've only come to bring, dear lad,
Your morning cup of tea.

'Last night I tucked you in your bed
So nice and warm and cosy,
Sang lullabies till you closed your eyes—
I hope your dreams were rosy.

'Perhaps you'd like your bath turned on?
Of course, you needn't hurry!
Just ring for breakfast when you please—
I want to save you worry!

'It is my dearest wish to be
A father to you boys.
Don't hesitate to bring to me
Your troubles and your joys.'

The Tommy thought: 'Am I in heaven
Among the angel folk?'
He sweetly smiled, just like a child.
And then, poor bloke, he woke.

EVADE WHO GETS PAID ON MONDAY AND IS BROKE BY WEDNESDAY WOULD LIKE TO EXCHANGE SMALL LOANS WITH AN EVADE WHO GETS PAID ON WEDNESDAY AND IS BROKE BY MONDAY.

Advertisement in MARKING TIME, the newspaper for escaped British POWs asylumed in Switzerland

The Aussie's Lament at Port Moresby

The man-eating mossies* of Moresby,
Their beaks are so big and so sharp,
That a nibble or two and you're just about through,
You may even be playing the harp.
We don't give a rap for the buggering Jap
We'll fight him like dinkum Aussies.
But Lord up above, if your children you love,
Why in HELL did you ever make mossies?

Iceland

We're Kensington boys from Kensington Gore
Who gave up our work because of the war:
And now we are sitting as snug as can be
On a little white island across the sea.

---

* Mosquitoes.

Oh a little bit of shit fell from the sky one day.
It landed in the ocean, so very far away,
And when the Air Force saw it, it looked so fucking bare,
They said, 'That's what we're looking for, we'll put the squadron there.'

Come to the cookhouse door, boys.
Dinner will be ready by and by.
If you haven't been to bed with the quarter-master's daughter
You can't have a second slice of pie.

Ashes to ashes and dust to dust,
If the Aussies don't get you, the Kiwis must.
We're moving on,
We're moving on,
Moving close to the shaking-up post,
We're moving on.

Dig ye Kiwis, dig like hell,
Here comes another Aussie shell.
We're moving on, *etc.*

In the following instructions to balloon barrage units, the word 'wench' was commonly substituted by a person unknown for the 'winch' of the original

1 Test purity. (Unless purity is below 50 per cent the operation is unlikely to be successful.)
2 Untie petticoat lacing and take off slip.
3 Bed down.

4 Inspect all apertures for wear.
5 Start up winch and close haul to point of attachment. (**NB** With new winches the point of attachment should be well greased.)
6 When winch is thoroughly warmed up, top up, using one-way filter. (Cane stiffener may be used, but should not be necessary.)
7 Repeat until storage drum is exhausted.
8 On bags.
9 Pay off winch.

Barrack-Room Intelligence

It was part of the job of education officers to instruct the other men in the nature of the enemy they were fighting.

This extract from a forces' newspaper in the east is an example of their efforts.

Q: What is hari-kiri? One chap in our hut says it's killing babies. I maintain it's sandbagging with sacks of rice.

A: Both wrong. Hari-kiri is Japanese art of suicide by laceration of stomach with sword or knife while guts slither out.

Japs with fat bellies have great advantage in making a good, workmanlike job of it. Slim Japs prefer meeting an honourable end by diving down volcanoes or mines. This method became so popular, and suicides so numerous, that tops of volancoes had to be fenced off and guards mounted to stop it. This was represented as a kill-joy measure.

ANTI HARA KIRI
GUARD

A Small Selection of Jokes from Forces' Newspapers

A sledge, seriously overladen with three Red Army staff officers and two British intelligence captains, lurched its way over the Siberian tundra.

Suddenly, they heard terrible howls behind them. Wolves! The horses were whipped up: but it was no use—the wolves caught up.

They threw their store of vodka overboard to gain extra speed, but it was not enough.

Finally, as the leading wolf made a leap for the sledge, the senior Russian officer, in the spirit of the east–west alliance, cried: 'My life for Comrade Stalin!' and leapt overboard.

The wolves gobbled him up as their hors d'oeuvres or zakousky, and were soon baying and howling around the sledge once more.

The second Russian stood up, saluted, shouted: 'Glory to the Red Army, the army of Lenin,' and hurled himself to the pack.

Still the wolves came, and the third Russian proclaimed: 'Up the USSR' before he, too, sacrificed himself.

With only the two British on board, the sledge gained speed: but the wolves were more than a match for the horses and kept up.

One of the Englishmen turned to the other and murmured, 'George, I think it's time you got out your Bren gun.'

The film star was vising a military hospital.

'Did you kill a Nazi?' she asked the occupant of the first bed she came to.

'Yes, lady,' he replied.

'Which hand did you use?'

'Me right 'and.'

The star took his right hand and gave it a lascivious kiss.

She went on to the next bed.

'I killed hundreds of them,' said the occupant.

'And which hand did you use?'

'I bit 'em to death,' he said.

Soldier, at Manchester Piccadilly Station, to guard: 'Is this train to London a corridor train?'

Guard: 'No, no corridor on this train.'

Soldier: 'That's done it. Where the hell am I going to stand?'

The sergeant-major went into the guardroom and found it deserted except for a private who, in his shirtsleeves and braces, was smoking a pipe.

'Where's the sergeant of the guard?' demanded the CSM.

'Gone across to the Sergeants' Mess for a drink,' was the reply.

'And the sentries?'

'In the canteen.'

'What in hell do you think you're doing here?'

'Me? I'm the prisoner.'

A major recommended a lance-corporal under his command for a commission.

After running the gamut of the psychologists and the selection board, the lance-corporal was returned to his unit as not being officer material.

Riled by this decision, the major borrowed the lance-corporal's uniform, and a week later presented himself before the Board.

Not only was he not recommended for a commission, but the Board suggested that it would be in the interests of the Army if he were deprived of his corporal's stripe.

'Say when,' said the Colonel to his ATS driver, pouring her a gin and tonic.

'One thing at a time, Colonel,' she replied. 'Let's have a drink first.'

D.Y.'s Cautionary Tales

Extensive inquiries have failed to unearth D.Y.'s identity.

So far as I can make out, he must have fought in North Africa, have been made a prisoner by the Germans and escaped from a German or Italian POW camp to Switzerland, where he wrote these very English verses, which I found stored in the British Museum.

Professor Voles, a Scientist who was only too successful

In Oxford, if you poke around,
Some rare old funnies may be found.
Turn but a stone, you start some bird
Whose name you've never even heard.
But who, as you'll discover later,
Makes Einstein look a selling-plater.

Just such a one was Herbert Voles,
Professor, Fellow of All Souls,
Who first, I understand, observed
That straight lines are not straight but curved
And that infinites have an end.
(His pupils thought him round the bend.)

To Voles another major war
Was just another major bore,
Till Whitehall cries 'There is one man
And only one alive who can
Twist beams about and, by deflection,
Send bombers in the wrong direction.'
Professor Voles, who answers 'True,
It is a simple thing to do.

I'll steer them anywhere you like.'
And then sets off upon his bike,
To No. 90 Woodstock Road,
Where he has his obscure abode
And lives on rusks and tonic waters
With seven truly ghastly daughters,
Whom he has sired, though when and how
He never can remember now.

That very night they came in force
And, having ascertained their course,
Professor Voles said, 'I will steer
Each enemy formation here,
An interesting experiment
To prove the beam's correctly bent.'
They met above the Woodstock Road
And then proceeded to unload
Their bombs, like men unloading coals:
That was the end of Herbert Voles,
His daughters and some 60 dons.
(All Souls put up a plaque, in bronze.)

Moral: Martyrs to science all consist
Of others than the scientist.

D.Y.

Colonel Fiennes, whose disbelief in modern weapons was his undoing

Our SMO, one Colonel Fiennes,
Displayed a great contempt for mines.
'Pooh! Pooh!' he'd say and also 'Pshaw!
I never heard of them before.
If they exist—and that I doubt—
They're nothing one need fuss about.
Just drive straight on—I always do—
And they will never injure you!'
As those who say of wasps: 'Keep still,
And it won't sting!' Oh yes it will.
But as with wasps the beastly mines,
Did show a tolerance of Fiennes,
Who kept on motoring to and fro,
Remarking 'See, I told you so!'
While left and right, trucks and their drivers
Were going up: the maimed survivors,
As they came limping into mess,
Could tolerate him less and less.
'I'd like to see,' you'd hear them sigh,
'The silly (Colonel) blown sky high!'
Th' Eumenides, slow at the gate,
Reserved their effort for the straight
And, full of running, overtook
The Colonel just outside Tobruk,
Where, as he bathed one day, he saw
A Horrid Object washed ashore,
With Horns before and Horns behind
Such as adorn—well, never mind.
A prey to curiosity
He cried 'Whatever can this be?'
There came a sudden warning shout,
'Hi! don't you muck that there about!'
Too late, a horn in either hand,
He'd started for a Better Land.

Moral: Ponder the fate of Colonel Fiennes
And don't you muck about with mines.

D.Y.

Mary Fry, whose carelessness cut short a promising career in espionage

The dearest wish of Mary Fry
Was to become a Female Spy,
And when they'd tested out her nerves
And measured up her various curves
The boys in MI5 said 'She
Is what a Female Spy should be:
As cold as ice, as hard as steel,
And yet how soft . . . Here, Colonel, feel,
A girl like this would get a Plan
From any normal, healthy man.'

Dressed in a simple Lanvin suit,
Mary was dropped by parachute
And made a perfect three-point landing
Just where Field-Marshal X was standing.
'*Himmel und Lieberwurst*,' cried he,
'Das ist indeed my cup of tea.
Achtung! and should the Führer phone,
Tell him I wish to be alone.'

Within a week of Mary's fall
The plans began to reach Whitehall.
A camisole, a brassiere,
From Stockholm forwarded by air,

Revealed, when warmed, to expert eyes,
Things calculated to surprise.
But as it was, our General Staff
Could sit and simply laugh and laugh.

Alas, the best of girls may trip
And Mary made a fatal slip.
If only she had faced her host
Or not worn what she'd meant to post.

Moral: A working girl can never be
Too careful of her lingerie.

D.Y.

Aubrey Poop, a victim of wander-lust and his brother St John, who wisely stayed at home

'What man who is a man at all
Could fail to hear the desert's call?'
Cried Aubrey Poop, 'The life for me
Is that of the LRDG.'
And doubtless such a life is grand
For those who like a lot of sand,
A lot of heat, a lot of flies,
A lot of Stukas in the skies.
But desert sands grow quickly cold
For men of less heroic mould
And, walking back towards Matruh,
With still 200 miles to do.
Hungry and tired, feet to hell,
In sight no single Bir (or well)
Said Aubrey, 'What a lousy place is
A desert without one oasis.

I must have been a silly fish
To venture west of Sidi Bish.'
Msus is where the Graves Commission
Have spotted Aubrey Poop's position.

Meanwhile his brother, St John Poop,
Had joined the *Short* Range Desert Group
Which keeps the Pyramids in sight
From Mena House on Sunday night
And based on Shepheards, moves no nearer
Wide open spaces than Gezireh.
Here St John proved a great success
And ran a really slap-up mess,
Which may explain, for all I know,
His Colonelcy and DSO.

Moral: If Arabs choose to, let them roam,
The prudent man will stay at home.

D.Y.

Of General Brett, who chose the wrong moment to be rude

Even in India, General Brett
Was famous as a martinet.
The real old school, pop-eyes and liver,
Whose very glance would make you shiver
While at his voice, now tiger's growl,
Now the bereaved hyena's howl.
Full Colonels, yes, and Brigadiers
Would blench and then collapse in tears.

At home, when 'Storm' gave place to 'Gale'
The very bearer's face grew pale,
The syces hid behind the stables,
The khidmagars beneath the tables
As came a startled cry from dhobi
'Memsahib, think Sahib got hydrophobi!'

Poor Memsahib—or, in English, wife—
The General led her such a life
It was no wonder she was dim
And went in awful dread of him
Or that their daughter, Ethel, seemed
As one who slept and, sleeping, dreamed
Of murder foul being done at night.
Poor little girl, she looked a sight.

'Twas thus with qualified regret
That India heard that General Brett
Was posted to the Middle East,
Which did not like him in the least.
From Port Sudan to Abbassia
They looked on him with hate and fear,
Until one day he broke the rule
You learn at any public school
Viz. 'Kick the boy below but love
And reverence the boy above.'
And at a hush-hush conference, graced
By someone Very Highly Placed,
Spoke out of turn. Well, that was that
They handed him a Bowler Hat,
All right in London, I daresay,
But not the headgear for Bombay.

Moral: When being offensive always try
To pick on those who daren't reply.

D.Y.

13

The Home Front

During World War II, there were two British points of view about Blighty—that of those who were conscripted to go abroad and defend it, and that of those who stayed behind.

The first section of the almost final part of this book represents the former point of view, and the second, the latter.

Blighty

We have heard about that island
With Aussies by the score,
Norwegians, Poles and Canadians,
And now the Yankees too.
We read of lonely outposts
Five miles from a town,
With only darts and wireless.
It really makes us frown.
We see upon the newsreel
Canadians doing their stuff.
Good shooting, Canadians,
It's only our fluff.
We are in the desert,
A grand place as you know,
And often talk and wonder
When it's their turn to have a go.

BLIGHTY

'We wonder if the language
Back home is just the same
And if the streets we know so well
Now bear a foreign name.'

I really think the weather
Out here would suit them fine.
Then they could broadcast to the world
They were really in the line.
We wonder if the language
Back home is just the same,
And if the streets we know so well
Now bear a foreign name.

Home Leave from the Desert

It's a man's place in this desert,
Where water can't be found,
Where Arabs follow one about
And lizards gather round.

It's a man's place in this desert,
Where sunshine hurts your eyes.
In fact, I think there's nothing worse
Than the sun, the sand, the flies.

It gets you, does the desert,
It gets you in the end.
You hate and loathe your fellow men.
You quarrel with your friend.

Your water ration seems so small,
The sun your temper tries.
It's an awful place in summer-time
With the sun, the sand, the flies.

The worst part of the desert
Are the sandstorms that abound.
They blow your bloody head off
And knock you to the ground.

The sand gets in your ears,
Your throat, your nose, your eyes.
It makes you keep on cussing at
The sun, the sand, the flies.

At last you leave this desert
And glad you are to go.
You are going to the homeland
Where sandstorms never blow.

Where people live in houses
And seem to be good guys.
Once there, you'll soon forget
The sun, the sand, the flies.

Then you reach old England
And strange enough you find
There is no thrill of welcome
From those you left behind.

The people, they seem strangers,
It's no use heaving sighs,
In fact, they're every bit as bad
As the sun, the sand, the flies.

The girls, they all seem crazy.
They drink and smoke and curse.
They seem to follow Yanks about
And go from bad to worse.

And therein lies the trouble
I'm telling you no lies,
In fact, I think I'd much prefer
The sun, the sand, the flies.

The home-fronters delighted in portraying to themselves through jokes and verses their phlegm in the face of air-raid warnings that interrupted them halfway through a pint of mild in the pub, food-rationing and the like.

Their good spirit is not to be disparaged. They had far more grievous things to complain about: but the ethic was to grouse about the lesser ones where possible.

Home-fronters liked to portray themselves, at least, as people who made their contribution towards winning the war by living the attitude represented by the following story.

A Huddersfield man, asked by a GI he met in a pub what he did when there was an air-raid, replied: 'Nowt. I reckon the Jerries have to take off some place across t'water. Then they have to find England. Then they have to find Huddersfield. Then they have to find Ramsbottom Road. Then they have to find the Lamb and Flag. And if they do, the chances are I'll be in the Rose and Crown all the time.'

The Anthem of the Ministry of Fuel and Power

If it's heat that you require,
Poke the missus, not the fire.
If you still want any more
Poke the little girl next door.
Poke all the fucking girls in town
But put that fucking poker down.

The Home Guard Song

To the tune of 'Not Last Night, but the Night Before'

Drunk last night, drunk the night before.
We're off to get drunk tonight, if we never get drunk no more.
The more we are, the merrier we shall be,
We are the lads of the LDV,*
Glorious, victorious, one barrel of beer between the four of us.
Glory to God there aren't any more of us.
For one of us could drink the fucking lot,
One of us could drink the fucking lot.

Special Instructions To Fire Watchers

1 One belt round waist with seven hooks to support three sandbags and four buckets of water.
2 One axe in belt.
3 One stirrup pump to be carried over left shoulder.
4 One extending ladder over right.
5 One whistle carried in mouth.
6 One long-handled shovel to be tucked under left arm.
7 Two wet blankets to be carried on head.
8 Spare sand to be carried in all pockets.
9 One box of matches to light any incendiary which fails to ignite.
10 One tin hat with turned-up brim to carry spare water.
11 One roll of toilet paper to be slung on the back ready for immediate use.

---

* Local Defence Volunteers.

Willie

Willie, in his roguish way,
Tipped grandma in the fire one day.
Mother said: 'My dear, that's cruel!
But of course it does save fuel.'

Tommy

Tommy, for his evening game
Set his sister's hair aflame.
The warden shouted at the sight:
'Wretched boy. PUT OUT THAT LIGHT.'

Shark Pie

'Shark was on sale at a Hampstead fish and poultry shop yesterday. It was selling at 1/3d a pound'—*News Item.*

How many fish and poultry shops
Have sharks behind the till.
But there's a fish and poultry shop
That stands on Hampstead Hill,
Which had one on the slab: it sold
At one-and-three a pound.
Which shows that mugs will always be
Where sharks are to be found.

Hugh Barty-King

14

Envoi

What is a Soldier?

'A soldier is a nobody,'
We hear lots of people say.
'He's an outcast in this world
And always in the way.'

We admit there are many bad ones,
From the army to the marines.
But you will find the majority
The best you have ever seen.

Most people condemn a soldier
When he takes a drink or two.
But does a soldier condemn you
When you've taken a decent few?

Now do not scorn a soldier,
But clasp him by the hand.
For the uniform he wears
Means protection for your land.

The Government picks the soldier
From millions far and wide.
So place him as your equal,
Real buddies, side by side.

When a soldier goes to battle
You cheer him on his way.
But he is never heard of,
When in his grave he lay.

But the greatest battle of a soldier
Comes in time of peace,
When people scorn and mock him
And treat him like a beast.

With these few lines we close, sir,
And hope we don't offend
So when you meet a soldier
Just treat him as your friend.

Oh let your songs be silent
And your voices mute.
A soldier's not an opera star.
He's just a bloody brute.

Index of Titles

Index of First Lines

PTE SM